The Problem of 'Edwin Drood'
A Study in the Methods of Dickens

W. Robertson Nicoll

Alpha Editions

This edition published in 2024

ISBN 9789362517593

Design and Setting By
Alpha Editions
www.alphaedis.com
Email - info@alphaedis.com

As per information held with us this book is in Public Domain.
This book is a reproduction of an important historical work.
Alpha Editions uses the best technology to reproduce historical work
in the same manner it was first published to preserve its original nature.
Any marks or number seen are left intentionally to preserve.

Contents

PREFACE	- 1 -
INTRODUCTION	- 4 -
PART I.—THE MATERIALS FOR A SOLUTION	- 5 -
CHAPTER I—THE TEXT OF EDWIN DROOD	- 6 -
CHAPTER II—EXTERNAL TESTIMONIES	- 16 -
CHAPTER III—THE ILLUSTRATIONS ON THE WRAPPER	- 46 -
CHAPTER IV—THE METHODS OF DICKENS	- 54 -
PART II—ATTEMPT AT A SOLUTION	- 66 -
CHAPTER V—WAS EDWIN DROOD MURDERED?	- 67 -
CHAPTER VI—WHO WAS DATCHERY?	- 82 -
CHAPTER VII—OTHER THEORIES	- 99 -
CHAPTER VIII—HOW WAS 'EDWIN DROOD' TO END?	- 102 -

PREFACE

The first serious discussion of *The Mystery of Edwin Drood* came from the pen of the astronomer, Mr. R. A. Proctor. Mr. Proctor wrote various essays on the subject. One appears in his *Leisure Readings*, included in Messrs. Longmans' 'Silver Library.' A second was published in 1887, and entitled *Watched by the Dead*. There were, I believe, in addition some periodical articles by Mr. Proctor; these I have not seen. Mr. Proctor modified certain positions in his earlier essay included in *Leisure Readings*, so that the paper must not be taken as representative of his final views. Whatever may be thought of Mr. Proctor's theory, all will admit that he devoted much care and ingenuity to the study, and that he had an exceptional knowledge of Dickens's books.

In 1905 Mr. Cuming Walters published his *Clues to Dickens's Mystery of Edwin Drood*. The *Athenæum* expressed its conviction 'that in these hundred pages or so he has found the clue, the main secret which had baffled all previous investigators, and so has secured permanent association with one of the immortals.' Mr. Cuming Walters's book was immediately followed by Mr. Andrew Lang's *The Puzzle of Dickens's Last Plot*. In this Mr. Lang adopted with modifications the theory of Mr. Proctor. The subject continued to interest this lamented author to the end of his life. He wrote many letters and articles on the theme, coming ultimately to the conclusion that Dickens did not know himself how his story was to be ended.

In 1910 Professor Henry Jackson of Cambridge published a volume, *About Edwin Drood*. It is a work of sterling merit, and particularly valuable for its study of the chronology of the story. Dr. Jackson was the first to examine the manuscript in a scholarly way, and to give some of the chief results. His conclusions are in the main those of Mr. Cuming Walters, but they are supported by fresh arguments and criticisms.

There have been many articles on the subject, particularly in that excellent periodical, the *Dickensian*, edited by Mr. B. W. Matz. Of this magazine it may be said that every number adds something to our knowledge of the great author.

By far the most successful attempt to finish the book is that of Gillan Vase, which was published in 1878. It is the only continuation worth looking at.

Among the best of the periodical contributions are those by Dr. M. R. James of Cambridge, published in the *Academy*, and in the *Cambridge Review*. The papers of Mr. G. F. Gadd in the *Dickensian* deserve special praise. In the *Bookman* Mr. B. W. Matz, whose knowledge of Dickens is unsurpassed, has declared for the view that Edwin Drood was murdered, but has not committed himself to any theory of Datchery.

I should not have been justified in publishing this volume if I had been able to add no new material. But I venture to think it will be found that while I have freely used the arguments and the discoveries of previous investigators, I have made a considerable addition to the stores. In particular, I have brought out the fact that Forster declined to accept Dickens's erasures in the later proofs, and I have printed the passages which Dickens meant to have omitted. The effect of the omissions is also traced to a certain extent, though not fully. The more one studies them, the more significant they appear.

I have printed completely for the first time the Notes and Plans for the novel. I have also published some notes on the manuscript based on a careful examination. These notes are not by any means complete, but they include perhaps the more important facts. Through the kindness of Miss Bessie Hatton and Mr. B. W. Matz I have been able to give an account of the unacted play by Charles Dickens the younger and Joseph Hatton on *Edwin Drood*.

I have also put together for the first time the external evidence on the subject. It is particularly important that this evidence should be read in full, and much of it is now inaccessible to the general reader. In the discussion of the main problems it will, I believe, be found that certain new arguments have been brought forward. In particular I ask attention to the quotations from the Bancroft *Memoirs* and from *No Name*. I have also given certain studies of the methods of Dickens which may be useful.

I have to acknowledge with warm thanks the kindness of Mr. Hugh Thomson in sending me his reading of the Wrapper.

It will thus, I hope, be found that the study is a contribution to the subject, and not a mere repetition or paraphrase of what has been advanced.

I have made no attempt at summarising the novel. No one can possibly attack the problem with any hope of success who has not read the book over and over again. A hasty perusal will serve no purpose. The fragment deserves and repays the very closest study.

There are questions that have been raised and arguments that have been stated which are not mentioned here. This is not because of ignorance. I have read, I believe, practically all that has been published on the theme. What I have omitted is matter that seems to me trivial or irrelevant.

While fully believing in the accuracy of the conclusions I have reached, I desire to avoid dogmatism. There is always the possibility that a writer may be diverted from his purpose. He may come to difficulties he cannot surmount. The fact that scholarly students of Dickens have come to different conclusions is a fact to be taken into account.

My thanks are due to Lord Rosebery for kindly accepting the dedication of the volume. Lord Rosebery is, however, in no way responsible for my arguments or my conclusions.

In preparing this study I have had the constant assistance and counsel of my accomplished colleague, Miss Jane T. Stoddart. Miss Stoddart's accuracy and learning and acuteness have been of the greatest use to me, and there is scarcely a chapter in the volume which does not owe much to her.

Mr. J. H. Ingram has most kindly furnished me with information about Poe.

Mr. Clement Shorter has allowed me to use his very valuable collection of newspaper articles.

Mr. B. W. Matz has very courteously answered some inquiries, and he has permitted me to use his valuable bibliography.

Messrs. Chapman & Hall have kindly given me permission to use the Wrapper, etc.

Mr. Cuming Walters has been so kind as to read the proofs.

If there are those who think that the problem does not deserve consideration, I am not careful to answer them. It is a problem which will be discussed as long as Dickens is read. Those who believe that Dickens is the greatest humorist and one of the greatest novelists in English literature, are proud to make any contribution, however insignificant, to the understanding of his works. Mr. Gladstone, in his 'Essay on the Place of Homer in Education,' mentions the tradition of Dorotheus, who spent the whole of his life in endeavouring to elucidate the meaning of a single word in Homer. Without fully justifying this use of time, we may agree in Mr. Gladstone's general conclusion 'that no exertion spent upon any of the classics of the world, and attended with any amount of real result, is thrown away.'

BAY TREE LODGE, HAMPSTEAD,
    Sept. 1912.

INTRODUCTION

The three mysteries of *Edwin Drood* are thus stated by Mr. Cuming Walters:

'The first mystery, partly solved by Dickens himself, is the fate of Edwin Drood. Was he murdered?—if so, how and by whom, and where was his body hidden? If not, how did he escape, and what became of him, and did he reappear?

'The second mystery is—Who was Mr. Datchery, the "stranger who appeared in Cloisterham" after Drood's disappearance?

'The third mystery is—Who was the old opium woman, called the Princess Puffer, and why did she pursue John Jasper?'

It is with the first two of these mysteries that this book is concerned. In the concluding chapter some hints are offered as to the third, but in my opinion there are no sufficient materials for any definite answer.

The problem before us is to decide with one half of Dickens's book in our possession what the course of the other half was likely to be.

It is important to lay stress upon this. An able reviewer in the *Athenæum*, 1st April 1911, says: 'The book is still in its infancy. Its predecessor, *Our Mutual Friend*, attained to some sixty-seven chapters, *Great Expectations* to fifty-nine, *Bleak House* to sixty-six. There is no strain on probability in supposing that *Edwin Drood* might, in happier circumstances, have reached something like these proportions.' The fact is that the book was to be completed in twelve numbers, and we have six.

In the first part of this volume I have dealt with the materials for a solution.

In the second part, I have used the materials and the internal evidence of the book, and attempted an answer to the questions.

PART I.—THE MATERIALS FOR A SOLUTION

CHAPTER I—THE TEXT OF EDWIN DROOD

The materials for the solution of the 'Edwin Drood' problems must first of all be found in the text of the unfinished volume. Hitherto it has not been observed that the book we have is not precisely what it was when Dickens left it. Three parts had been issued by Dickens himself. After his death the remaining three parts were issued by John Forster. Dickens had corrected his proofs up to and including chapter xxi. The succeeding chapters xxii. and xxiii. are untouched. I discovered to my great surprise on examining the proofs in the Forster Collection that Forster had in every case ignored Dickens's erasures, and had replaced all the omitted passages in the text. Thus it happens that we do not read the book as Dickens intended us to read it. We have passages which on consideration he decided not to print. It is unnecessary to criticise the action of Forster, but it seems clear that he should at least have given warning to the reader. I now print the passages erased by Dickens and restored by Forster.

SENTENCES AND PARTS OF SENTENCES ERASED BY DICKENS

In Chapter XVII.:—

> *an eminent public character, once known to fame as Frosty faced Fogo,*

> *by, always, as it seemed, on errands of antagonistically snatching something from somebody, and never giving anything to anybody.*

> *'Sir,' said Mr. Honeythunder, in his tremendous voice, like a schoolmaster issuing orders to a boy of whom he had a bad opinion, 'sit down.'*

> *Mr. Crisparkle seated himself.*

> *Mr. Honeythunder having signed the remaining few score of a few thousand circulars, calling upon a corresponding number of families without means to come forward, stump up instantly, and be Philanthropists, or go to the Devil, another shabby stipendiary Philanthropist (highly disinterested, if in earnest) gathered these into a basket and walked off with them.*

when they were alone,

Mr. Crisparkle rose, a little heated in the face, but with perfect command of himself.

'Mr. Honeythunder,' he said, taking up the papers referred to: 'my being better or worse employed than I am at present is a matter of taste and opinion. You might think me better employed in enrolling myself a member of your Society.'

'Ay, indeed, sir!' retorted Mr. Honeythunder, shaking his head in a threatening manner. 'It would have been better for you if you had done that long ago!'

'I think otherwise.'

'Or,' said Mr. Honeythunder, shaking his head again, 'I might think one of your profession better employed in devoting himself to the discovery and punishment of guilt than in leaving that duty to be undertaken by a layman.'

'Perhaps I expect to retain it still?' Mr. Crisparkle returned, enlightened; 'do you mean that too?'

'Well, sir,' returned the professional Philanthropist, getting up and thrusting his hands down into his trousers pockets, 'I don't go about measuring people for caps. If people find I have any about me that fit 'em, they can put 'em on and wear 'em, if they like. That's their look out: not mine.'

It seems a little hard to be so tied to a stake, and innocent; but I don't complain.'

'And you must expect no miracle to help you, Neville,' said Mr. Crisparkle, compassionately.

'No, sir, I know that.

and that of course I am guiding myself by the advice of such a friend and helper. Such a good friend and helper!'

He took the fortifying hand from his shoulder, and kissed it. Mr. Crisparkle beamed at the books, but not so brightly as when he had entered.

But they were as serviceable as they were precious to Neville Landless.

'I don't think so,' said the Minor Canon. 'There is duty to be done here; and there are womanly feeling, sense, and courage wanted here.'

'I meant,' explained Neville, 'that the surroundings are so dull and unwomanly, and that Helena can have no suitable friend or society here.'

'You have only to remember,' said Mr. Crisparkle, 'that you are here yourself, and that she has to draw you into the sunlight.'

They were silent for a little while, and then Mr. Crisparkle began anew.

'When we first spoke together, Neville, you told me that your sister had risen out of the disadvantages of your past lives as superior to you as the tower of Cloisterham Cathedral is higher than the chimneys of Minor Canon Corner. Do you remember that?'

'Right well.'

'I was inclined to think it at the time an enthusiastic flight. No matter what I think it now. What I would emphasise is, that under the head of Pride your sister is a great and opportune example to you.'

'Under all heads that are included in the composition of a fine character, she is.'

'Say so; but take this one.'

She can dominate it even when it is wounded through her sympathy with you.

Every day and hour of her life since Edwin Drood's disappearance, she has faced malignity and folly—for you—as only a brave nature well directed can. So it will be with her to the end.

which knows no shrinking, and can get no mastery over her.'

as she is a truly brave woman,'

As Mr. Grewgious had to turn his eye up considerably before he could see the chambers, the phrase was to be taken figuratively and not literally.

'A watch?' repeated Mr. Grewgious musingly.

'I entertain a sort of fancy for having him under my eye to-night, do you know?'

In Chapter XVIII.

'indeed, I have no doubt that we could suit you that far, however particular you might be.

with a general impression on his mind that Mrs. Tope's was somewhere very near it, and that, like the children in the game of hot boiled beans and very good butter, he was warm in his search when he saw the Tower, and cold when he didn't see it.
He was getting very cold indeed when. 'Until' is put in here.

'Indeed?' said Mr. Datchery, with a second look of some interest.

Mr. Datchery, taking off his hat to give that shock of white hair of his another shake, seemed quite resigned, and betook himself whither he had been directed.

Perhaps Mr. Datchery had heard something of what had occurred there last winter?

Mr. Datchery had as confused a knowledge of the event in question, on trying to recall it, as he well could have. He begged Mrs. Tope's pardon when she found it incumbent on her to correct him in every detail of his summary of the facts, but pleaded that he was merely a single buffer getting through life upon his means as idly as he could, and that so many people were so constantly making away with so many other people, as to render it difficult for a buffer of an easy temper to preserve the circumstances of the several cases unmixed in his mind.

'Might I ask His Honour,' said Mr. Datchery, 'whether that gentleman we have just left is the gentleman of whom I have heard in the neighbourhood as being much afflicted by the loss of a nephew, and concentrating his life on avenging the loss?'

'That is the gentleman. John Jasper, sir.'

'Would His Honour allow me to inquire whether there are strong suspicions of any one?'

'More than suspicions, sir,' returned Mr. Sapsea; 'all but certainties.'

'Only think now!' cried Mr. Datchery.

'But proof, sir, proof must be built up stone by stone,' said the Mayor. 'As I say, the end crowns the work. It is not enough that Justice should be morally certain; she must be immorally certain—legally, that is.'

'His Honour,' said Mr. Datchery, 'reminds me of the nature of the law. Immoral. How true!'

'As I say, sir,' pompously went on the Mayor, 'the arm of the law is a strong arm, and a long arm. That is the way I put it. A strong arm and a long arm.'

'How forcible!—And yet, again, how true!' murmured Mr. Datchery.

'And without betraying what I call the secrets of the prison-house,' said Mr. Sapsea; 'the secrets of the prison-house is the term I used on the bench.'

> '*And what other term than His Honour's would express it?*' said Mr. Datchery.
>
> '*Without, I say, betraying them, I predict to you, knowing the iron will of the gentleman we have just left (I take the bold step of calling it iron, on account of its strength), that in this case the long arm will reach, and the strong arm will strike. This is our Cathedral, sir. The best judges are pleased to admire it, and the best among our townsmen own to being a little vain of it.*'
>
> *All this time Mr. Datchery had walked with his hat under his arm, and his white hair streaming.*

In the next sentence the word *now* is struck out.

> '*He had an odd momentary appearance upon him of having forgotten his hat, when Mr. Sapsea now touched it.*'

> '*I shall come. Master Deputy, what do you owe me?*'
>
> '*A job.*'
>
> '*Mind you pay me honestly with the job of showing me Mr. Durdles's house when I want to go there.*'

In Chapter XX.:—

> '*Yes, you may be sure that the stairs are fireproof,*' said Mr. Grewgious, '*and that any outbreak of the devouring element would be perceived and suppressed by the watchmen.*'

In Chapter XXI.:—

> *I wished at the time that you had come to me; but now I think it best that you did as you did, and came to your guardian.*'
>
> '*I did think of you,*' Rosa told him; '*but Minor Canon Corner was so near him—*'
>
> '*I understand. It was quite natural.*'

'Have you settled,' asked Rosa, appealing to them both, 'what is to be done for Helena and her brother?'

'Why really,' said Mr. Crisparkle, 'I am in great perplexity. If even Mr. Grewgious, whose head is much longer than mine, and who is a whole night's cogitation in advance of me, is undecided, what must I be!'

Am I agreed with generally in the views I take?'

'I entirely coincide with them,' said Mr. Crisparkle, who had been very attentive.

'As I have no doubt I should,' added Mr. Tartar, smiling, 'if I understood them.'

'Fair and softly, sir,' said Mr. Grewgious; 'we shall fully confide in you directly, if you will favour us with your permission.'

I begin to understand to what you tend,' said Mr. Crisparkle, 'and highly approve of your caution.'

'I needn't repeat that I know nothing yet of the why and wherefore,' said Mr. Tartar, 'but I also understand to what you tend, so let me say at once that my chambers are freely at your disposal.'

THE MANUSCRIPT

I make also a few notes based on a careful examination of the manuscript. Certain passages are rewritten, and the result pasted over the original page. These passages have been noted. Also certain sentences have been altered in form, sometimes by the substitution of one word for another, and sometimes by the addition of words. It is not necessary to give every example, but a few may be noted.

Towards the end of the second chapter the passage beginning 'I have been taking opium for a pain,' including the long paragraph which follows, has been entirely rewritten and pasted on.

In the description of the Landlesses in chapter vi. Dickens made certain changes. As the sentence stands now it reads as follows: 'An unusually handsome lithe young fellow, and an unusually handsome lithe girl; much alike; both very dark, and very rich in colour; she of almost the gipsy type; something untamed about them both; a certain air upon them of hunter and huntress; yet withal a certain air of being the objects of the chase, rather than the followers.'

As originally written it read thus: 'A handsome young fellow, and a handsome girl; both dark and rich in colour; she quite gipsy like; something untamed about them both; a certain air upon them of hunter and huntress; yet a certain air of being the objects of the chase, rather than the followers.'

In chapter vii., where Neville is speaking of his sister, as we have the passage it reads: 'In a last word of reference to my sister, sir (we are twin children), you ought to know, to her honour, that nothing in our misery ever subdued her, though it often cowed me. When we ran away from it (we ran away four times in six years, to be soon brought back and cruelly punished), the flight was always of her planning and leading. Each time she dressed as a boy, and showed the daring of a man. I take it we were seven years old when we first decamped; but I remember, when I lost the pocket-knife with which she was to have cut her hair short, how desperately she tried to tear it out, or bite it off.'

The original version ran thus: 'In reference to my sister, sir (we are twin children), you ought to know, to her honour, that nothing in our misery ever cowed her, though it often cowed me. When we ran away from it (we ran away four times in five years, to be very soon brought back and punished), the flight was always of her planning. Each time she dressed as a boy, and showed the daring of a man. I take it we were eight years old when we first decamped; but I remember, when I lost the pocket-knife with which she was to have cut her hair short, that she tried to tear it out, or bite it off.'

At the beginning of chapter xviii. we read of the stranger in Cloisterham: 'Being buttoned up in a tightish blue surtout.' This was originally: 'Being dressed in a tightish blue surtout.' A little further on in the same paragraph we have: 'He stood with his back to the empty fireplace.' Dickens originally wrote: 'He stood with his back to the fireplace.' In the next paragraph 'His shock of white hair' was originally 'His shock of long white hair.'

In the same chapter, when Datchery and the boy are standing looking at Jasper's rooms we have the following sentence: '"Indeed?" said Mr. Datchery, with a second look of some interest.' This was originally written: '"Indeed?" said Mr. Datchery, with an appearance of interest.' In the final proofs this passage was entirely struck out. On the next page we have this sentence: 'Mr. Datchery, taking off his hat to give that shock of white hair of his another shake, seemed quite resigned, and betook himself whither he had been directed.' The original version ran thus: 'Mr. Datchery, taking off his hat and giving his shock of white hair another shake, was quite resigned, and betook himself whither he had been directed.'

A little further on in the same chapter, when Datchery first goes into Jasper's room we have: '"I beg pardon," said Mr. Datchery, making a leg with his hat under his arm.' This was originally written, "I beg pardon," said Mr. Datchery, hat in hand.'

In the last paragraph of this chapter we have: 'Said Mr. Datchery to himself that night, as he looked at his white hair in the gas-lighted looking-glass over the coffee-room chimney-piece at the Crozier, and shook it out: "For a single buffer, of an easy temper, living idly on his means, I have had a rather busy afternoon!"' This was originally written: 'Said Mr. Datchery to himself that night as he looked at his white hair in the gas-lighted looking-glass over the coffee-room chimney-piece at the Crozier: "Well, for a single buffer of an easy temper, living idly on his means, I have had rather a busy afternoon!"'

In chapter xx., when Grewgious is talking about Bazzard we have the following: '"No, he goes his way, after office hours. In fact, he is off duty here, altogether, just at present; and a firm downstairs, with which I have business relations, lend me a substitute. But it would be extremely difficult to replace Mr. Bazzard."' Originally Dickens wrote: '"No, he goes his ways after office hours. In fact, he is off duty at present; and a firm downstairs with which I have business relations, lend me a substitute. But it would be difficult to replace Mr. Bazzard."'

Chapter xxii. is much corrected, and the whole of the second paragraph is rewritten and pasted on. Chapter xxiii. is also a good deal corrected. Near the beginning we have the following: 'The Cathedral doors have closed for the night; and the Choir-master, on a short leave of absence for two or three services, sets his face towards London.' This was originally written: 'The Cathedral doors have closed for the night; and the Choir-master, on leave of absence for a few days, sets his face towards London.'

The passage beginning: 'But she goes no further away from it than the chair upon the hearth,' and the next two paragraphs are entirely rewritten and pasted on, and the following sentences are cancelled: '"So far I might a'most as well have never found out how to set you talking," is her commentary. "You are too sleepy to talk too plain. You hold your secrets right you do!"' A little further on we have: '"Halloa!" he cries in a low voice, seeing her brought to a standstill: "who are you looking for?"' This was originally '"Halloa!" cries this gentleman, "who are you looking for?"'

On the next page we have: 'With his uncovered gray hair blowing about.' Dickens originally wrote: 'With his gray hair blowing about.'

On the same page, when Datchery and the opium woman are talking together Dickens puts in the following sentence about opium as an afterthought: '"And it's like a human creetur so far, that you always hear what can be said against it, but seldom what can be said in its praise."'

A little further on we have: 'Mr. Datchery stops in his counting, finds he has counted wrong, shakes his money together, and begins again.' Originally we had: 'Mr. Datchery stops in his counting, finds he has counted wrong, and begins again.' Very near the end of this chapter we have: 'At length he rises, throws open the door of a corner cupboard, and refers to a few uncouth chalked strokes on its inner side.' Dickens first wrote: 'At length he rises, throws open the door of a corner cupboard, and refers to a few chalked strokes on its inner side.'

CHAPTER II—EXTERNAL TESTIMONIES

We now proceed to give such external testimony as exists of the plans and intentions of Dickens. The chief authority is, of course, the *Life* by Forster. We have in addition the testimony of Madame Perugini, whose first husband, Charles Allston Collins, designed the wrapper. To this we add the testimony of Charles Dickens the younger as conveyed to his sister. Through the kindness of Miss Bessie Hatton I have been able to read the text of the unacted play written by Joseph Hatton and Charles Dickens the younger on *The Mystery of Edwin Drood*. We have also the important letter of Sir Luke Fildes, who was chosen by Dickens to illustrate the story. It seems essential to any complete consideration of the subject that these testimonies should be given in full, and this is the more necessary because some of them are now not readily at hand.

JOHN FORSTER'S TESTIMONY

Dickens in 1868 had been alarming his friends and exhausting himself by his public Readings. When he was in America on his last Reading tour he had made a profit of about £20,000. He entered into an agreement with Messrs. Chappell to give a final course of Readings in this country, from which he expected to receive an additional £13,000. The strain of his work in America had manifestly told upon him. 'There was manifest abatement of his natural force, the elasticity of bearing was impaired, and the wonderful brightness of eye was dimmed at times.' Unfavourable and alarming symptoms of nerve mischief were also noted, but he drew lavishly on his reserve strength, and thinking that a new excitement was needed he chose the *Oliver Twist* murder, one of the most trying of his public recitals. He suffered 'thirty thousand shocks to the nerves' going to Edinburgh. His Readings and his journeyings exacted from him the most terrible physical exertion, but no warnings could arrest his course till his physicians peremptorily ordered him to desist. Even then, however, he resumed his Readings at a later date.

In this condition of mental and bodily fatigue Dickens began his last book. I print almost in full the relative passages from Forster.

> The last book undertaken by Dickens was to be published in illustrated monthly numbers, of the old form, but to close with the twelfth. It closed, unfinished, with the sixth number, which was itself underwritten by two pages.

His first fancy for the tale was expressed in a letter in the middle of July. 'What should you think of the idea of a story beginning in this way?—Two people, boy and girl, or very young, going apart from one another, pledged to be married after many years—at the end of the book. The interest to arise out of the tracing of their separate ways, and the impossibility of telling what will be done with that impending fate.' This was laid aside; but it left a marked trace on the story as afterwards designed, in the position of Edwin Drood and his betrothed.

I first heard of the later design in a letter dated 'Friday, the 6th of August 1869,' in which, after speaking, with the usual unstinted praise he bestowed always on what moved him in others, of a little tale he had received for his journal, he spoke of the change that had occurred to him for the new tale by himself. 'I laid aside the fancy I told you of, and have a very curious and new idea for my new story. Not a communicable idea (or the interest of the book would be gone), but a very strong one, though difficult to work.' The story, I learnt immediately afterward, was to be that of the murder of a nephew by his uncle; the originality of which was to consist in the review of the murderer's career by himself at the close, when its temptations were to be dwelt upon as if, not he, the culprit, but some other man, were the tempted. The last chapters were to be written in the condemned cell, to which his wickedness, all elaborately elicited from him as if told of another, had brought him. Discovery by the murderer of the utter needlessness of the murder for its object, was to follow hard upon commission of the deed; but all discovery of the murderer was to be baffled till towards the close, when, by means of a gold ring which had resisted the corrosive effects of the lime into which he had thrown the body, not only the person murdered was to be identified, but the locality of the crime and the man who committed it. So much was told to me before any of the book was written; and it will be recollected that the ring, taken by Drood to be given to his betrothed only if their engagement went on, was brought away with him from their last interview. Rosa was to marry Tartar, and Crisparkle the sister of Landless, who was himself, I think, to have perished in assisting Tartar finally to unmask and seize the murderer.

Nothing had been written, however, of the main parts of the design excepting what is found in the published numbers; there was no hint or preparation for the sequel in any notes of chapters in advance; and there remained not even what he had himself so sadly written of the book by Thackeray also interrupted by death. The evidence of matured designs never to be accomplished, intentions planned never to be executed, roads of thought marked out never to be traversed, goals shining in the distance never to be reached, was wanting here. It was all a blank. Enough had been completed nevertheless to give promise of a much greater book than its immediate predecessor. 'I hope his book is finished,' wrote Longfellow, when the news of his death was flashed to America. 'It is certainly one of his most beautiful works, if not the most beautiful of all. It would be too sad to think the pen had fallen from his hand, and left it incomplete.' Some of its characters are touched with subtlety, and in its descriptions his imaginative power was at its best. Not a line was wanting to the reality, in the most minute local detail, of places the most widely contrasted; and we saw with equal vividness the lazy cathedral town and the lurid opium-eater's den. Something like the old lightness and buoyancy of animal spirits gave a new freshness to the humour; the scenes of the child-heroine and her luckless betrothed had both novelty and nicety of character in them; and Mr. Grewgious in chambers with his clerk and the two waiters, the conceited fool Sapsea, and the blustering philanthropist Honeythunder, were first-rate comedy. Miss Twinkleton was of the family of Miss La Creevy; and the lodging-house keeper, Miss Billickin, though she gave Miss Twinkleton but a sorry account of her blood, had that of Mrs. Todgers in her veins. 'I was put in early life to a very genteel boarding-school, the mistress being no less a lady than yourself, of about your own age, or it may be some years younger, and a poorness of blood flowed from the table which has run through my life.' Was ever anything better said of a school-fare of starved gentility?

The last page of *Edwin Drood* was written in the châlet in the afternoon of his last day of consciousness; and I have thought there might be some interest in a facsimile of the greater part of this final page of manuscript that ever came from his hand, at which he had worked unusually late in order to finish the chapter. It has very much the character, in its excessive care of correction and interlineation, of all his later manuscripts; and in order that comparison may be made with his earlier and easier method, I place beside it a portion of a page of the original of *Oliver Twist*. His greater pains and elaboration of writing, it may be mentioned, become first very obvious in the later parts of *Martin Chuzzlewit*; but not the least remarkable feature in all his manuscripts is the accuracy with which the portions of each representing the several numbers are exactly adjusted to the space the printer has to fill. Whether without erasure or so interlined as to be illegible, nothing is wanting, and there is nothing in excess. So assured had the habit become, that we have seen him remarking upon an instance the other way, in *Our Mutual Friend*, as not having happened to him for thirty years. Certainly the exceptions had been few and unimportant; but *Edwin Drood* more startlingly showed him how unsettled the habit he most prized had become, in the clashing of old and new pursuits. 'When I had written' (22nd of December 1869), 'and, as I thought, disposed of the first two numbers of my story, Clowes informed me to my horror that they were, together, *twelve printed pages too short*! Consequently I had to transpose a chapter from number two to number one, and remodel number two altogether. This was the more unlucky, that it came upon me at the time when I was obliged to leave the book, in order to get up the Readings' (the additional twelve for which Sir Thomas Watson's consent had been obtained); 'quite gone out of my mind since I left them off. However, I turned to it and got it done, and both numbers are now in type. Charles Collins has designed an excellent cover.' It was his wish that his son-in-law should have illustrated the story; but this not being practicable, upon an opinion expressed by Mr. Millais which the result thoroughly justified, choice was made of Mr. S. L. Fildes.

Forster goes on to explain as follows the discovery of the manuscript containing the passage 'How Mr. Sapsea Ceased to be a Member of the Eight Club.' This is to be found in every edition of *Edwin Drood*, but Forster's remarks are important and must be reproduced:

This reference to the last effort of Dickens's genius had been written as it thus stands, when a discovery of some interest was made by the writer. Within the leaves of one of Dickens's other manuscripts were found some detached slips of his writing, on paper only half the size of that used for the tale, so cramped, interlined, and blotted as to be nearly illegible, which on close inspection proved to be a scene in which Sapsea the auctioneer is introduced as the principal figure, among a group of characters new to the story. The explanation of it perhaps is, that, having become a little nervous about the course of the tale, from a fear that he might have plunged too soon into the incidents leading on to the catastrophe, such as the Datchery assumption in the fifth number (a misgiving he had certainly expressed to his sister-in-law), it had occurred to him to open some fresh veins of character incidental to the interest, though not directly part of it, and so to handle them in connection with Sapsea as a little to suspend the final development even while assisting to strengthen it. Before beginning any number of a serial, he used, as we have seen in former instances, to plan briefly what he intended to put into it chapter by chapter; and his first number-plan of *Drood* had the following: 'Mr. Sapsea. Old Tory jackass. Connect Jasper with him. (He will want a solemn donkey by and by)'; which was effected by bringing together both Durdles and Jasper, for connection with Sapsea, in the matter of the epitaph for Mrs. Sapsea's tomb. The scene now discovered might in this view have been designed to strengthen and carry forward that element in the tale; and otherwise it very sufficiently expresses itself. It would supply an answer, if such were needed, to those who have asserted that the hopeless decadence of Dickens as a writer had set in before his death. Among the lines last written by him, these are the very last we can ever hope to receive; and they seem to me a delightful specimen of the power possessed by him in his prime, and the rarest which any novelist can have, of revealing a character by a touch. Here are a couple of people, Kimber and Peartree, not known to us before, whom we read off thoroughly in a dozen words; and as to Sapsea himself, auctioneer and mayor of Cloisterham, we are face to face with what before we only dimly realised, and we see the solemn jackass, in his business pulpit, playing off the airs of Mr. Dean in his Cathedral pulpit, with Cloisterham laughing at the impostor.'

MADAME PERUGINI'S TESTIMONY

Madame Perugini's article appeared in the *Pall Mall Magazine* for June 1906. The title is 'Edwin Drood and the Last Days of Charles Dickens, by his younger daughter Kate Perugini.' Madame Perugini begins by summarising the evidence of Forster as already given. She proceeds to make the following instructive comments. It will be observed also that she makes no additions to the external evidence, particularly on the vexed question of the wrapper:

> *The Mystery of Edwin Drood* is a story, or, to speak more correctly, the half of a story, that has excited so much general interest and so many speculations as to its ultimate disclosures, that it has given rise to various imaginary theories on the part of several clever writers; and to much discussion among those who are not writers, but merely fervent admirers and thoughtful readers of my father's writings. All these attach different meanings to the extraordinary number of clues my father has offered them to follow, and they are even more keen at the present day than they were when the book made its first appearance to find their way through the tangled maze and arrive at the very heart of the mystery. Among the numerous books, pamphlets, and articles that have been written upon *Edwin Drood*, there are some that are extremely interesting and well worth attention, for they contain many clever and possible suggestions, and although they do not entirely convince us, yet they add still more to the almost painful anxiety we all feel in wandering through the lonely precincts of Cloisterham Cathedral, or along the banks of the river that runs through Cloisterham town and leads to the Weir of which we are told in the story.
>
> In following these writers to the end of their subtle imaginings as to how the mystery might be solved, we may sometimes be inclined to pause for an instant and ask ourselves whether my father did not perhaps intend his story to have an ending less complicated, although quite as interesting, as any that are suggested. We find ourselves turning to John Forster's *Life of Charles Dickens* to help us in our perplexity, and this is what we read in his chapter headed 'Last Book.' Mr. Forster begins by telling us that

Edwin Drood was to be published in twelve illustrated monthly parts, and that it closed prematurely with the sixth number, which was itself underwritten by two pages; therefore my father had exactly six numbers and two pages to write when he left his little châlet in the shrubbery of Gad's Hill Place on 8th June 1870, to which he never returned. Mr. Forster goes on to say: 'His first fancy for the tale was expressed in July (meaning the July of 1869), in a letter which runs thus:

'"What should you think of the idea of a story beginning in this way?—Two people, boy and girl, or very young, going apart from one another, pledged to be married after many years—at the end of the book. The interest to arise out of the tracing of their separate ways and the impossibility of telling what will be done with that impending fate."'

This idea my father relinquished, although he left distinct traces of it in his tale; and in a letter to Mr. Forster, dated 6th August 1869, tells him:

'I laid aside the fancy I told you of, and have a very curious and new idea for my new story. Not a communicable idea (or the interest of the book would be gone), but a very strong one, though difficult to work.'

Mr. Forster then says that he immediately afterwards learnt that the story was to be 'the murder of a nephew by his uncle'; the originality of which was to consist in the review of the murderer's career by himself at the close, when its temptations were to be dwelt upon as if not he, the culprit, but some other man, were the tempted. The last chapters were to be written in the condemned cell, to which his wickedness, all elaborately elicited from him as if told of another, had brought him. Discovery by the murderer of the utter needlessness of the murder for its object, was to follow hard upon commission of the deed; but all discovery of the murderer was to be baffled till towards the close, when, by means of a gold ring which had resisted the corrosive effects of the lime into which he had thrown the body, not only the person murdered was to be identified, but the locality of the crime and the man who committed it.'

Mr. Forster adds a little information as to the marriages at the close of the book, and makes use of the expression 'I think' in speaking of Neville Landless, as though he were not quite certain of what he remembered concerning him. This 'I think' has been seized upon by some of Mr. Forster's critics, who appear to argue that because he did not clearly recollect one detail of the story he may therefore have been mistaken in the whole. But we see for ourselves that Mr. Forster is perfectly well informed as to the nature of the plot, and the fate of the two principal characters concerned, the murdered and the murderer; and the only thing upon which he is not positive is the ending of Neville Landless, to which he confesses in the words 'I think,' thus making his testimony to the more important facts the more impressive. If we have any doubts as to whether Mr. Forster correctly stated what he was told, we have only to turn to the story of *Edwin Drood*, and we find, as far as it goes, that his statement is entirely corroborated by what we read in the book.

If those who are interested in the subject will carefully read what I have quoted, they will not be able to detect any word or hint from my father that it was upon the Mystery alone that he relied for the interest and originality of his idea. The originality was to be shown, as he tells us, in what we may call the psychological description the murderer gives us of his temptations, temperament, and character, as if told by another; and my father speaks openly of the ring to Mr. Forster. Moreover, he refers to it often in his story, and we all recognise it, whatever our other convictions may be, as the instrument by which Jasper's wickedness and guilt are to be established in the end. I do not mean to imply that the mystery itself had no strong hold on my father's imagination; but, greatly as he was interested in the intricacies of that tangled skein, the information he voluntarily gave to Mr. Forster, from whom he had withheld nothing for thirty-three years, certainly points to the fact that he was quite as deeply fascinated and absorbed in the study of the criminal Jasper, as in the dark and sinister crime that has given the book its title. And he also speaks to Mr. Forster of the murder of a nephew by an uncle. He does not say that he is uncertain whether he shall save the nephew, but has evidently made up his mind that the crime is to be committed. And so he told his plot to Mr. Forster, as he had been accustomed to tell his plots for years past; and those who knew him must feel it impossible to believe that in this, the last year of his life, he should suddenly become underhand, and we might say treacherous, to his old friend, by inventing for his private edification a plot that he had no intention of carrying into execution. This is incredible, and the nature of the friendship that existed between Mr. Forster and himself makes the idea unworthy of consideration.

Mr. Forster was devotedly attached to my father, but as years passed by this engrossing friendship made him a little jealous of his confidence, and more than a little exacting in his demands upon it. My father was perfectly aware of this weakness in his friend, and although the knowledge of it made him smile at times, and even joke about it when we were at home and alone, he was always singularly tenderhearted where Mr. Forster was concerned, and was particularly careful never to wound the very sensitive nature of one who, from the first moment of their acquaintance, had devoted his time and energy to making my father's path in life as smooth as so intricate a path could be made. In all business transactions Mr. Forster acted for him, and generally brought him through these troubles triumphantly, whereas, if left to himself, his impetuosity and impatience might have spoilt all chances of success; while in all his private troubles my father instinctively turned to his friend, and even when not invariably following his advice, had yet so much confidence in his judgment as to be rendered not only uneasy but unhappy if Mr. Forster did not approve of the decision at which he ultimately arrived. From the beginning of their friendship to the end of my father's life the relations between the two friends remained unchanged; and the notion that has been spread abroad that my father wilfully misled Mr. Forster in what he told him of the plot of *Edwin Drood* should be abandoned, as it does not correspond with the knowledge of those who understood the dignity of my father's character, and were also aware of the perfectly frank terms upon which he lived with Mr. Forster.

If my father again changed his plan for the story of *Edwin Drood* the first thing he would naturally do would be to write to Mr. Forster and inform him of the alteration. We might imagine for an instant that he would perhaps desire to keep the change as a surprise for his friend, but what I have just stated with regard to Mr. Forster's character renders this supposition out of the question, as my father knew for a certainty that his jealousy would debar him from appreciating such a surprise, and that he would in all probability strongly resent what he might with justice be allowed to consider as a piece of unnecessary caution on my father's part. That he did not write to Mr. Forster to tell him of any divergence from his second plan for the book we all know, and we know also that my eldest brother, Charles, positively declared that he had heard from his father's lips that Edwin Drood was dead. Here, therefore, are two very important witnesses to a fact that is still doubted by those who never met my father, and were never impressed by the grave sincerity with which he would have given this assurance.

It is very often those who most doubt Mr. Forster's accuracy on this point who are in the habit of turning to his book when they are in the search of facts to establish some theory of their own; and they do not hesitate to do this, because they know that whatever views they may hold upon the work itself, or the manner in which it is written, absolute truth is to be found in its pages. Why should they refuse, therefore, to believe a statement made upon one page of his three volumes, when they willingly and gratefully accept the rest if it is to their interest to do so? This is a difficult question to answer, but it is not without importance when we are discussing the subject of *Edwin Drood*. On pages 425 and 426 of the third volume of Mr. Forster's *Life* is to be found the simple explanation of my father's plot for his story, as given to him by my father himself. It is true that Mr. Forster speaks from remembrance, but how often does he not speak from remembrance, and yet how seldom are we inclined to doubt his word? Only here, because what he tells us does not exactly fit in with our preconceived views as to how the tale shall be finished, are we disposed to quarrel with him, for the simple reason that we flatter ourselves we have discovered a better ending to the book than the one originally intended for it by the author. And so we put his statement aside and ignore it, while we grope in the dark for a thing we shall never find; and we obstinately refuse to allow even the little glimmer of light my father has himself thrown upon the obscurity to help us in our search. It was not, I imagine, for the intricate working out of his plot alone that my father cared to write this story; but it was through his wonderful observation of character, and his strange insight into the tragic secrets of the human heart, that he desired his greatest triumph to be achieved.

I do not write upon these things because I have any fresh or startling theories to offer upon the subject of *Edwin Drood*. I cannot say that I am without my own opinions, but I am fully conscious that after what has been already so ably said, they would have but little interest for the general public; so I shrink from venturing upon any suggestions respecting the solution of my father's last book. My chief object in writing is to remind the readers of this paper that there are certain facts connected with this story that cannot lightly be put aside, and these facts are to be found in John Forster's *Life of Charles Dickens*, and in the declaration made by my brother Charles. Having known both Mr. Forster and my brother intimately, I cannot for a moment believe that either of them would speak or write that which he did not know to be strictly true; and it is on these grounds alone that I think I have a right to be heard when I insist upon the assertion that Edwin Drood was undoubtedly murdered by his uncle Jasper. As to the unravelling of the mystery, and the way in which the murder was perpetrated, we are all at liberty to have our own views, seeing that no explanations were as yet arrived at in the story; but we should remember that only vague speculations can be indulged in when we try to imagine them for ourselves.

It has been pointed out, and very justly, that although Jasper removed the watch, chain, and scarf-pin from Edwin's body, there would possibly remain on it money of some kind, keys, and the metal buttons on his clothes, which the action of the quicklime could not destroy, and by which his identity would be made known. This has been looked upon as an oversight, a mere piece of forgetfulness on my father's part. But remembering, as I do very well, what he often said, that the most clever criminals were constantly detected through some small defect in their calculations, I cannot but think it most probable that this was not an oversight, but was intended to lead up to the pet theory that he so frequently mentioned whenever a murder case was brought to trial. After reading *Edwin Drood* many times, as most of us have read it, we must, I think, come to the conclusion that not a word of this tale was written without full consideration; that in this story at least my father left nothing to chance, and that therefore the money, and the buttons, were destined to take their proper place in the book, and might turn out to be a weak spot in Jasper's well-arranged and complicated plot, *the* weak spot my father insisted upon, as being inseparable from the commission of a great crime, however skilfully planned. The keys spoken of need not be taken seriously into account, for Edwin was a careless young fellow, and it is not unreasonable to suppose that he did not always carry them upon his person; he was staying with his uncle, and he may have left them in the portmanteau, which was most likely at the time of the murder lying unfastened in his room, with the key belonging to it in the lock. It would be unfair to suggest that my father wrote unadvisedly of this or that, for he had still the half of his story to finish, and plenty of time, as he thought, in which to gather up the broken threads and weave them into a symmetrical and harmonious whole, which he was so eminently capable of completing.

That my father's brain was more than usually clear and bright during the writing of *Edwin Drood*, no one who lived with him could possibly doubt; and the extraordinary interest he took in the development of this story was apparent in all that he said or did, and was often the subject of conversation between those who anxiously watched him as he wrote, and feared that he was trying his strength too far. For although my father's death was sudden and unexpected, the knowledge that his bodily health was failing had been for some time too forcibly brought to the notice of those who loved him, for them to be blind to the fact that the book he was now engaged in, and the concentration of his devotion and energy upon it, were a tax too great for his fast-ebbing strength. Any attempt to stay him, however, in work that he had undertaken was as idle as stretching one's hands to a river and bidding it cease to flow; and beyond a few remonstrances now and again urged, no such attempt was made, knowing as we did that it would be entirely useless. And so the work sped on, carrying with it my father's few remaining days of life, and the end came all too soon, as it was bound to come, to one who never ceased to labour for those who were dear to him, in the hope of gaining for them that which he was destined never to enjoy. And in my father's grave lies buried the secret of his story.

The scene of the Eight Club, which Mr. Forster discovered after his death, in which there figure two new characters, Mr. Peartree and Mr. Kimber, bears no relation as we read it to the unfolding of the plot; and although the young man Poker, who is also introduced in this fragment for the first time, seems to be of more significance, we see too little of him to be certain that we may not already have made his acquaintance. In Mr. Sapsea my father evidently took much pleasure, and we are here reminded of the note made for him in the first number-plan of *Edwin Drood*: 'Mr. Sapsea. Old Tory jackass. Connect Jasper with him. (He will want a solemn donkey by and by.)' My father also wanted the solemn donkey, and not only brought him in for the purposes of his story, but because, as in the case of 'the Billickin,' he took delight in dwelling upon the absurdities of the character.

As to the cover of *Edwin Drood*, that has been the subject of so much discussion there is very little to tell. It was designed and drawn by Mr. Charles A. Collins, my first husband. The same reasons that prevented me from teasing my father with questions respecting his story made me refrain from asking any of Mr. Collins; but from what he said I certainly gathered that he was not in possession of my father's secret, although he had made his designs from my father's directions. There are a few things in this cover that I fancy have been a little misunderstood. In the book only Jasper and Neville Landless are described as dark young men. Edwin Drood is fair, and so is Crisparkle. Tartar is burnt by the sun; but when Rosa asks 'the Unlimited head chambermaid' at the hotel in Furnival's Inn if the gentleman who has just called is dark, she replies:

'No, Miss, more of a brown gentleman.'

'You are sure not with black hair?' asked Rosa, taking courage.

'Quite sure of that, Miss. Brown hair and blue eyes.'

Now in a drawing it would be difficult to make a distinction between the fair hair of Edwin and the slightly darker hair of Tartar; and in the picture, where we see a girl—Rosa we imagine her to be—seated in a garden, the young man at her feet is, I feel pretty sure, intended for Tartar. Edwin it cannot be, nor Neville, as has been supposed, for he was decidedly dark. Besides this, Neville would not have told his affection to Rosa, for Helena was far too quick-witted not to understand from Rosa's first mention of Tartar that she is already in love with him, and she would have warned and saved the brother to whom she was so ardently attached from making any such confession. The figure is not intended for Jasper, because we know that Jasper did not move from the sun-dial in the scene where he declares his mad passion for Rosa, and Jasper had black hair and whiskers. And, again, the drawing cannot be meant to represent Helena and Crisparkle, for the young man is not in clerical dress. The figures going up the stairs are still more difficult to make out; but there can be little doubt that the active higher one is the same young man we see at Rosa's feet, and must therefore be Tartar. Of the remaining two, one may be Crisparkle, although there is still no clerical attire, and the other either Grewgious or Neville, though the drawing certainly bears but little resemblance to either of those characters.

The lower and middle picture is, of course, the great scene of the book; but whether the young man standing calm, and inexorable as Fate, is intended to be the ghost of Edwin as seen by Jasper in his half-dazed and drugged condition, or whether it is Helena dressed as Datchery, as one writer has ingeniously suggested (although there are reasons in the story against the supposition that Helena is Datchery, and many to support the theory that the 'old buffer' is Bazzard),—these are puzzles that will never be cleared up, except to the minds of those who have positively determined that they hold the clue to the mystery, and can only see its interpretation from one point of view. The girl's figure with streaming hair, in the picture where the word 'Lost' is written, has been supposed to represent Rosa after her parting from Edwin; but it may more likely, I think, indicate some scene in the book which has yet to be described in the story. This is another enigma; but my father, it may be presumed, intended to puzzle his readers by the cover, and he had every legitimate right to do so, for had his meaning been made perfectly clear 'the interest of the book would be gone.' Some surprise has been expressed because Mr. Forster did not ask Mr. Collins for the meaning of his designs; but if he already knew the plot, why should he seek information from Mr. Collins? particularly as my father may have told him that he had not disclosed the secret of his story to his illustrators, for I believe I am right in affirming that Mr. Luke Fildes was no better informed as to the plan of the book than was Mr. Collins.

I am unfortunately not acquainted with much that has been written about *Edwin Drood*, for the story was so painfully associated with my father's death and the sorrow of that time that after first reading it I could never bear to look into the book again till about two months ago, when I found myself obliged to do so; and then my thoughts flew back to the last occasion when my father mentioned it in my hearing.

. . . . .

There is one other fact connected with my father and *Edwin Drood* that I think my readers would like to know, and I must be forgiven if I again speak from my own experience in order to relate it. Upon reading the book once more, as I have already told, after an interval of a great number of years, the story took such entire possession of me that for a long time I could think of nothing else; and one day, my aunt, Miss Hogarth, being with me, I asked her if she knew anything more definite than I did as to how the ending was to be brought about. For I should explain that when my father was unusually reticent we seldom, if ever, attempted to break his silence by remarks or hints that might lead him to suppose that we were anxious to learn what he had no doubt good reasons for desiring to keep from us. And we made it a point of honour among ourselves never, in talking to him on the subject of *Edwin Drood*, to show the impatience we naturally felt to arrive at the end of so engrossing a tale.

My aunt said that she knew absolutely nothing, but she told me that shortly before my father's death, and after he had been speaking of some difficulty he was in with his work, without explaining what it was, she found it impossible to refrain from asking him, 'I hope you haven't really killed poor Edwin Drood?' To which he gravely replied, 'I call my book the Mystery, not the History, of Edwin Drood.' And that was all he would answer. My aunt could not make out from the reply, or from his manner of giving it, whether he wished to convey that the Mystery was to remain a mystery for ever, or if he desired gently to remind her that he would not disclose his secret until the proper time arrived for telling it. But I think his words are so suggestive, and may carry with them so much meaning, that I offer them now, with my aunt's permission, to those who take a delight in trying to unravel the impenetrable secrets of a story that has within its sadly shortened pages a most curious fascination, and is 'gifted with invincible force to hold and drag.'

THE TESTIMONY OF CHARLES DICKENS THE YOUNGER

I have quoted from Madame Perugini's statement the words: 'We know also that my elder brother Charles positively declared that he had heard from his father's lips that Edwin Drood was dead.' I proceed to corroborate the statement by giving here a brief account of the play by Joseph Hatton and Charles Dickens.

The importance of this play as a witness to Dickens's intentions is shown in an article by Joseph Hatton which appeared in the *People* on 19th November 1905. Mr. Hatton explains that about the year 1880, in a conversation, he sketched out his idea of the play up to the crucial point. Dickens had a play in his mind when he wrote the story, and it was said that he had thought of Dion Boucicault as his collaborator in his work for the stage. After the death of Dickens, Boucicault had a mind to write the play and invent his own conclusion to the story, but afterwards gave it up. Mr. Hatton, in a conversation with Mr. Luke Fildes, saw Dickens's possible conclusion, but did not attempt to gather up the broken threads. 'Consulting his son, Charles, to whom I offered my sketch, I found that his father had revealed to him sufficient of the plot to clearly indicate how the story was to end. We agreed to write the play. Much of the son's version of the finale was proved by the instructions which the author had given to the illustrator in regard to certain of the unpublished and unwritten chapters. And so Dickens the younger and I fell to work and wrote the play of *Edwin Drood* for the Princess's Theatre.' He goes on to explain that the piece was cast, and a great point made of the authoritative conclusion of the story, thus clearing up something of the mystery which was part of its title. But Mr. Harry Jackson, the stage manager, did not like the play, and it was left unacted. Years after, Dickens had a hope that Mr. Willard would undertake the play, but this expectation was not fulfilled. Dickens consoled himself by saying that next to the pleasure of having a good play acted was the pleasure of writing it, and for the rest he took the incident as one of the 'little ironies' of his life.

The play as it lies before me is in four Acts. The first is made up of conversations between the Landlesses, Mrs. Crisparkle, Septimus Crisparkle, Rosa and Edwin. These are practically repeated from the book. Grewgious and Jasper then come on the scene, the novel being closely followed in their conversation. The second Act is made up of conversations also mainly reproduced from the book between Helena and Rosa, Jasper and Crisparkle. Grewgious comes on in the second Scene where Edwin and Rosa decide to be brother and sister. There follow in the third Scene the talks between Jasper and Durdles. Edwin talks to the opium woman, and Jasper appears with the scarf on his arm. So far there is practically nothing that is not taken directly from Dickens. The third Act opens with a conversation between Septimus and Mrs. Crisparkle as to the guilt of Landless. Helena and Neville appear protesting innocence. Grewgious tells Jasper about the breaking of the engagement between Edwin and Rosa. Jasper makes love to Rosa. In the concluding Act the scene is laid in the opium den in London: 'Dark, poverty-stricken. Fourpost bedstead, chair, table, candlestick, set well down so as to allow good space for vision later on, light up a little, when Opium Sal lights candle shortly after Jasper's entrance. For details see Fildes's picture in book. Opium Sal discovered moving about in a witch-like kind of way.' Jasper enters and tells Sal that a man followed him to the door. She lights the opium pipe for him, and then questions him.

He says at last: 'Hush! the journey's made! It's over!'

>SAL. Is it over so soon?

>JASPER. I must sleep that vision off. It is the poorest of all. No struggle, no consciousness of peril, no entreaty, and yet I never saw *that* before!

SAL. See what, deary?

JASPER. Look at it! Look what a poor miserable thing it is! *That* must be real. It's over.

(*He has accompanied this incoherence with some wild unmeaning gestures; but they trail off into the progressive inaction of stupor, and he lies like a log upon the bed. The* WOMAN *attempts to rouse him as before, but finding him past rousing for the time, she slowly gets upon her feet with an air of disappointment, flicks his face with her hand savagely, and then flings a rug over* JASPER.)

(*Both* SAL *and* JASPER *now being perfectly quiet, the back of scene is illuminated, showing the scene exactly as at end of Act II. The candle is out in the Opium Den, leaving front part of stage dark. The brightest light in vision is from* JASPER'S *window, leaving other parts of scene slightly in shadow but sufficiently light for action to be seen. It is to be carefully noted that all the persons on in the Vision Scene should wear list shoes, so that they make no noise in moving about, and that the Stage Manager should insist upon perfect quiet behind the stage and at the wings. The actors, too, speak in rather a measured, monotonous tone. Crowd later on in Vision to be grouped and drilled from this point of view.*)

(*The Scene being well open, there is a flash of lightning, and a peal of thunder, followed after a short pause by a burst of merry laughter from* JASPER'S *room, the voices of* DROOD *and* NEVILLE *being audible. They come down to door,* JASPER *with them, without his hat.*)

Edwin, Jasper, and Neville are talking. Edwin says he will walk with Neville as far as the river and have a look at the storm. Neville and Jasper exchange good-nights, and Edwin says: 'Don't go to bed, Jack, I won't be long.'

(JASPER *in response waves hand. Pause. Then re-enters house, closes door. Goes upstairs. Puts light out, and is seen for a moment at window. Flash of lightning, peal of thunder. Pause.* JASPER *comes out with hat on head, the black silk scarf on arm. Comes out cautiously, closing door after him and looks round, and warily goes to crypt; finds door locked and takes key from his pocket with which he opens it, and pushes door wide open. Creeps off in the direction* NEVILLE *and* EDWIN *have gone. Pause. Weak flash of lightning and peal of thunder.* JASPER *returns crouching, and hides within shadow of wall. Re-enter* EDWIN DROOD *from where exit was made. He looks up at* JASPER'S *window.*)

Ah, too bad; he has gone to bed and has put his light out.

(JASPER *rushes upon* EDWIN *from behind, seizes him, whips scarf, which he has previously been twisting into rope-like shape, round his head and neck, and proceeds to strangle him. There is a fierce struggle for a few seconds. Nearly on the point of death,* EDWIN *gets free of* JASPER, *sees his assailant, and thinks* JASPER *is there to help him.*)

EDWIN. Jack! Jack! Save me! They are killing me! (*Flings himself into* JASPER'S *arms.*)

JASPER. Save you, yes!

(*Deliberately tightens scarf, strikes* EDWIN, *and kills him. Flash of lightning and peal of thunder, as* EDWIN *falls lifeless at* JASPER'S *feet. Pause.*)

JASPER (*a little overcome physically, and jerking out his sentences gasping, but with intense ferocity*). You poor fool. You'll boast no more. (*Spurning body with his foot.*) Ah! ah! ah! (*Laughs wildly.*) He's gone. The fellow-traveller has gone for ever, gone down, into the everlasting abyss! Hush! (*Listens.*) Durdles? No, opium mixed with his liquor keeps that other fool quiet. (*Listens again, and looks cautiously round—distant low-moaning peal of thunder.*) Only the storm wearing itself out! Ah! ah! ah! (*Looking at body.*) You've seen the last of the storm, weak, self-satisfied fool! Come (wildly seizing the body, and dragging it towards crypt), come—to your marriage bed (*drags body*). Come—to sleep with Death!

(*Exit with body into crypt.*)

(*Slow music. Short pause. Re-enter* JASPER *from crypt, and as he does so gauze clouds begin to darken scene.* JASPER *locks crypt, puts key in his pocket, crosses, crouching and creeping, looking behind him fearfully, and enters his own house, with flash of lightning, peal of thunder, the very last of the storm. By this time gauze clouds nearly darken the scene. Double on bed moves.* OPIUM SAL *rises restlessly, once more leans over bed, and begins to talk while the actor representing* JASPER *returns to his place on bed.*)

SAL. Troubled dreams, deary! Troubled dreams. Have you been taking the journey again? Was it pleasant, and what did you do to fellow-traveller, eh?

JASPER (*speaking in a dreamy way*). That's how the journey was made—that's how I like to make it. But there's something more. I never saw that before; what is it? (*Fearfully, falls asleep again.*)

(SAL *wearily resumes her attitude of rest with her arms on bed, and the Vision Scene goes on.* DURDLES *appears beckoning off, unlocks crypt and enters. As he does so* GREWGIOUS *and* ROSA *come on from direction indicated by* DURDLES'S *beckoning, all the others in scene coming from the same place.* ROSA *clings to her guardian's arm. They stop in centre of stage opposite crypt, looking towards door.* NEVILLE *and* HELENA *follow. They join* GREWGIOUS *and* ROSA. CRISPARKLE *and* OPIUM SAL'S *Double come on.* OPIUM SAL'S *Double is pointing towards* ROSA *and others, and* CRISPARKLE *joins the group. The Double now stands near wing and beckons off. Townspeople come on and make group, Double at their head, she pointing towards crypt; they all look in that direction.* DURDLES *comes to door, beckons* GREWGIOUS, *who goes in after* DURDLES *to crypt. Groups now move a step or two nearer to entrance of crypt. Slight pause.* ROSA *clings to* HELENA; NEVILLE *in dumb show whispers anxiously to* HELENA *and* ROSA, *as if to reassure and comfort them.* HELENA *stands proudly but anxious;* ROSA *droopingly.*)

GREW. (*standing just outside crypt door, and addressing himself to* CRISPARKLE). Keep the women back; this is no place for them. Edwin Drood has been foully murdered!

(*Sensation in crowd, not indicated by noise, but dumb show.* ROSA *staggers.* NEVILLE *catches her in his arms.* JASPER *moves and groans in his sleep.* DURDLES *comes out of crypt, plucks* GREWGIOUS *by the sleeve, and holds up* JASPER'S *long black scarf.*)

CRIS. Jasper's scarf!

(JASPER *again groans on bed.*)

Where is Jasper?

(*Goes to door of* JASPER'S *house and knocks. This knocking must be made right at back of stage.*)

GREW. It is no good knocking there. The murderer of Edwin Drood will be found in London!

(*Sensation as before in crowd.* CRISPARKLE *still knocks, and between knocks faint rapping is heard at door of opium den, and*

JASPER *tosses about on bed, then starts up with a cry, the Vision disappearing the moment he stands on the floor.*)

JASPER (*starting as if at what he has seen*). No, no. It's a lie!

(*Knocking at opium den door becomes louder.*)

(*Turning to* SAL, *who is now at other end of room.*) What's that?

SAL. They wants to come in.

JASPER. Who wants to come in?

(*Knocking is louder and louder.*)

SAL. Why, the perlice.

JASPER. The police! Damnation! The man who followed me here to-night! Then it's all true. Durdles has found the body in spite of all my precautions, and I am lost. (Rushes wildly about room.) Is there no escape? Where's the window?

SAL. There ain't no winder, deary.

JASPER. Then I'm trapped like a wolf in a cage. You filthy hag, this is your doing.

(*Seizes candlestick on stool to strike her, she crouches down. Knocking at door now so fierce as to arrest his attention, and he turns towards it, weapon in his hand.*)

(*Voice at door.* Open in the Queen's name!)

(JASPER *drops stool or whatever he has seized upon to attack* SAL *with, staggers back, tears open his shirt-sleeve, where a small phial is seen fastened to left wrist, drags it from his wrist and holds it convulsively in right hand, as door is violently burst open.*)

(*Enter* Inspector of Police, *handcuffs in hand,* DURDLES, NEVILLE, CRISPARKLE, *and* GREWGIOUS.)

GREW. (*to* Officer, *pointing to* JASPER). There is your prisoner.

JASPER. Never! Do you think I was not prepared for this always! (*Takes poison, and flings phial down.*) Now I defy you! Hush! I did kill him! Ha! ha! The fellow-traveller! Yes. For love. For a mad wild passion. Killed him as I would have killed you and you—as I would have swept you all from the path that led to her. Ha! ha! what fools you were not to see it, not to see my love, how it burned, how it consumed me. She knew it! Rosa knew it. (*Then speaking as though none but he and* ROSA *were present.*) Rosa! Rosa! My Rosa! Come! You must! You shall! (*Wildly.*) Back! Back! She's mine I tell you! (*Passes hand over eyes, and staggers, then once more half realises the situation.*) What's that? (*Looks round, and sees* NEVILLE.) You here! You who think to reap the harvest for which I have sold my soul to hell! Vile wretch! I'll kill you!

(*Rushes to* NEVILLE, *who stands forward. In act of raising arm to strike him,* JASPER *is seized with death spasm, trembles, shudders, and, flinging up arms, falls dead. Picture:* OPIUM SAL *crouching still in fear, Officer,* GREWGIOUS, DURDLES, NEVILLE, *and* CRISPARKLE *near the body.*)

END OF DRAMA

THE TESTIMONY OF SIR LUKE FILDES

A reviewer in the *Times* Literary Supplement, 27th October 1905, wrote: 'Nor do we attach much importance to any of the hints Dickens dropped, whether to John Forster, to any member of his family, or to either of his illustrators. He was very anxious that his secret should not be guessed, and the hints which he dropped may very well have been intentionally misleading.' This called forth the following letter from Sir Luke Fildes:

TO THE EDITOR OF THE TIMES

Sir,—In an article entitled 'The Mysteries of Edwin Drood' in your issue of to-day, the writer, speculating on the various theories advanced as solutions of the mystery, ventures to say:—

'Nor do we attach much importance to any of the hints Dickens dropped, whether to John Forster, to any member of his family, or to either of his illustrators. He was very anxious that his secret should not be guessed, and the hints which he dropped may very well have been intentionally misleading.'

I know that Charles Dickens was very anxious that his secret should not be guessed, but it surprises me to read that he could be thought capable of the deceit so lightly attributed to him.

The 'hints he dropped' to me, his sole illustrator—for Charles Collins, his son-in-law, only designed the green cover for the monthly parts, and Collins told me he did not in the least know the significance of the various groups in the design; that they were drawn from instructions personally given by Charles Dickens, and not from any text—these 'hints' to me were the outcome of a request of mine that he would explain some matters, the meaning of which I could not comprehend, and which were for me, his illustrator, embarrassingly hidden.

I instanced in the printers' rough proof of the monthly part sent to me to illustrate where he particularly described John Jasper as wearing a neckerchief of such dimensions as to go twice round his neck; I called his attention to the circumstance that I had previously dressed Jasper as wearing a little black tie once round the neck, and I asked him if he had any special reasons for the alteration of Jasper's attire, and, if so, I submitted I ought to know. He, Dickens, appeared for the moment to be disconcerted by my remark, and said something meaning he was afraid he was 'getting on too fast' and revealing more than he meant at that early stage, and after a short silence, cogitating, he suddenly said, 'Can you keep a secret?' I assured him he could rely on me. He then said, 'I must have the double necktie! It is necessary, for Jasper strangles Edwin Drood with it.'

I was impressed by his earnestness, as indeed, I was at all my interviews with him—also by the confidence which he said he reposed in me, trusting that I would not in any way refer to it, as he feared even a chance remark might find its way into the papers 'and thus anticipate his "mystery"'; and it is a little startling, after more than thirty-five years of profound belief in the nobility of character and sincerity of Charles Dickens, to be told now that he probably was more or less of a humbug on such occasions.—I am, Sir, yours obediently,

LUKE FILDES.

HARROGATE, *October* 27.

NOTES FOR THE NOVEL

I give here the notes which Dickens made for his novel. These are partly quoted by Professor Jackson in his book,

About Edwin Drood, but are now for the first time printed complete.

Friday, Twentieth August 1869

	Gilbert Alfred.
	Edwin.
	Jasper Edwyn.
	Michael Oswald.
The Loss of James Wakefield.	Arthur.
Edwyn.	Selwyn.
	Edgar.
	Mr. Honeythunder.
	Mr. Honeyblast.
James's Disappearance.	The Dean.
	Mrs. Dean.
FLIGHT AND PURSUIT.	Miss Dean.

SWORN TO AVENGE IT.

ONE OBJECT IN LIFE.

A KINSMAN'S DEVOTION.

THE TWO KINSMEN.

The Loss of Edwyn Brood.

The Loss of Edwin Brude.

The Mystery in the Drood Family.

The Loss of Edwyn Drood.

The Flight of Edwyn Drood. Edwin Drood in hiding.

The Loss of Edwin Drude.

The Disappearance of Edwin Drood.

The Mystery of Edwin Drood.

Dead? or Alive?

Opium-Smoking.

 Touch the key-note.

  'When the wicked man—'

The Uncle & Nephew.

  'Pussy's' Portrait.

  You won't take warning then?

Dean.	Mr. Jasper.
Minor Canon, Mr. Crisparkle.	
Uncle & Nephew.	Verger.
Gloves for the Nuns' House.	Peptune.
Churchyard.	*Change to Tope.*

CATHEDRAL TOWN RUNNING THROUGHOUT.

Inside the Nuns' House.

 Miss Twinkleton and her double existence.

Mrs. Tisher.

Rosebud.

The affianced young people. *Every love scene after is a quarrel more or less.*

Mr. Sapsea.   Old Tory Jackass.

    His Wife's Epitaph.

Jasper and the Keys.

 Durdles down in the crypt and among the graves. His dinner bundle.

(*MYSTERY OF EDWIN DROOD.—NO. I.*)

CHAPTER I

THE DAWN

    change title to THE DAWN.

    opium smoking and Jasper.

    Lead up to Cathedral.

CHAPTER II

A DEAN AND A CHAPTER ALSO

| Cathedral & Cathedral Town | Mr. Crisparkle. |

and the Dean.

    Uncle & Nephew.

    Murder very far off.

Edwin's Story & Pussy.

CHAPTER III

THE NUNS' HOUSE

Still picturesque suggestions of Cathedral Town.

The Nuns' House and the young couple's first love scene.

CHAPTER IV

MR. SAPSEA

Connect Jasper with him. (He will want a solemn donkey by & by.)

    Epitaph brings them together, and brings Durdles with them.

    The Keys.   Story Durdles.

Bring in the other young couple.   YES

    Neville and Olympia Heyridge or Heyfort?

Neville & Helena Landless.

    Mixture of Oriental blood—or imperfectly acquired mixture in them. YES.

No

(*MYSTERY OF EDWIN DROOD.—NO. II.*)

CHAPTER V

PHILANTHROPY IN MINOR CANON CORNER

| The Blustrous Philanthropist. Mr. Honeythunder. | Old Mrs. Crisparkle. China Shepherdess. Minor Canon Corner. |

CHAPTER VI

MORE CONFIDENCES THAN ONE

Neville's to Mr. Crisparkle.

| Rosa's to Helena. | Piano scene with Jasper. She singing; he following her lips. |

CHAPTER VII

DAGGERS DRAWN

QUARREL.

(Fomented by Jasper). Goblet. And then confession to Mr. Crisparkle. *Jasper lays his ground.*

CHAPTER VIII

MR. DURDLES AND FRIEND

Deputy engaged to stone Durdles nightly.

Carry through the woman of the 1st chapter.

Carry through Durdles calling—and the bundle & the keys.

John Jasper looks at Edwin asleep.

Pursue Edwin Drood and Rosa?

Lead on to final scene then in No. V? IV?

Yes.

How many more scenes between them?

Way to be paved for their marriage and parting instead. *Yes.*

Miss Twinkleton's?   No.   Next No.

Rosa's Guardian?   DONE IN No. II.

Mr. Sapsea?   In last chapter.

Neville Landless at Mr. Crisparkle's

and Helena? YES.

Neville admires Rosa. That comes out from himself.

(*MYSTERY OF EDWIN DROOD. NO. III.*)

CHAPTER X [63]

SMOOTHING THE WAY

That is, for Jasper's plan, through Mr. Crisparkle who takes new ground on Nevill's new confidence.

Minor Canon Corner. The closet?

remember there is a child.

 Edwin's appointment for Xmas Eve.

CHAPTER XI

A PICTURE AND A RING

P.

J. T.

1747

| Drood in chambers. | [The two waiters] |

 Bazzard the clerk.

 Mr. Grewgious's past story:

'A ring of diamonds and rubies delicately set in gold.'

Edwin takes it.

CHAPTER XII

A NIGHT WITH DURDLES

Lay the ground for the manner of the murder to come out at last.

  Keep the boy suspended.

  Night picture of the Cathedral.

Once more carry through Edwin and Rosa?

  or Last time? LAST TIME.

 Then

Last meeting of Rosa & Edwin outside the Cathedral? YES.

  Kiss at parting.

  'Jack.'

Edwin goes to the dinner.

 The Windy night.

  The Surprise and Alarm.

  Jasper's failure in the one great

 object made known by Mr. Grewgious.

  Jasper's Diary? YES.

(*MYSTERY OF EDWIN DROOD.—NO. IV.*)

CHAPTER XIII

BOTH AT THEIR BEST

The Last Interview

   And Parting.

CHAPTER XIV

WHEN SHALL THESE THREE MEET AGAIN?

How each passes the day.

[Watch & shirt pin] [all Edwin's Jewellery.]	Neville. Edwin. Jasper.	[Watch to the Jewellers.]

'And so *he* goes up the Postern Stair.'

Storms of wind.

CHAPTER XV

IMPEACHED

Neville away cart. Pursued & brought back.

Mr. Grewgious's communication:

And his scene with Jasper.

CHAPTER XVI

DEVOTED

Jasper's artful use of the communication on his recovery.

Cloisterham Weir, Mr. Crisparkle, and the watch and pin.

Jasper's artful turn.

 The DEAN. Neville cast out.

  Jasper's Diary 'I devote myself to his destruction.'

Edwin and Rosa for the last time? DONE ALREADY.

Kinfederel.

Edwin Disappears.

THE MYSTERY. DONE ALREADY.

(MYSTERY OF EDWIN DROOD.—NO. V.)

CHAPTER XVII

PHILANTHROPY PROFESSIONAL AND UNPROFESSIONAL

CHAPTER XVIII

SHADOW ON THE SUN DIAL [67a]

A SETTLER IN CLOISTERHAM

CHAPTER XIX

A SETTLER IN CLOISTERHAM [67b]

SHADOW ON THE SUN DIAL

CHAPTER XX

LET'S TALK [67c]

VARIOUS FLIGHTS [67d] DIVERS FLIGHTS

(MYSTERY OF EDWIN DROOD.—NO. VI.)

CHAPTER XXI

A GRITTY STATE OF THINGS COMES ON

CHAPTER XXII

THE DAWN AGAIN

CHAPTER XXIII

CHAPTER III—THE ILLUSTRATIONS ON THE WRAPPER

Much attention has been given to the illustrations on the wrapper and their significance. So far as I can find, the question was first raised in the *Spectator*. On 1st October 1870, in a review of the first edition of *Edwin Drood*, the *Spectator* complained that the publishers had not given a facsimile of the vignetted cover. The critic proceeds: 'By whom was the lamplight discovery of a standing figure, apparently meant for Edwin Drood, in the vignette at the bottom of the page, intended to be made?' He inquired also whether the man entering with the lanthorn was John Jasper, and what were the directions given by Mr. Dickens as to the ascent of the winding staircase represented on the right hand of the cover. The *Spectator* asked for any authentic indications which might exist of the turn which Dickens intended to give to the story. 'Nor can we see how it can be possible that no such indications exist, with this prefiguring cover to prove that he had not only anticipated, but disclosed to some one or other, many of the situations he intended to paint.' Since then others, and in particular Mr. Andrew Lang, have with much insistency declared that the bottom picture represents a meeting of the risen Edwin Drood with his horror-stricken uncle, John Jasper.

In reply to these questions certain considerations may be adduced:

1. We have already shown from the testimony of Charles Allston Collins, as reported by his widow, and by Sir Luke Fildes, that he, at least, was not aware of any such intention in the mind of Dickens. On the contrary, Madame Perugini and Sir Luke Fildes are convinced that Edwin Drood was murdered. More than this, Charles Dickens the younger, who was more or less in his father's confidence, agreed with them. As we have noted, he affirmed that his father had told him that Edwin Drood was murdered, and he constructed his play on that basis.

2. I attach much weight to Madame Perugini's suggestion that whatever her father meant or did not mean, he was certainly not the man to give away on the cover the answer to the mystery. He may have meant—he very probably did—before he began the story to mystify his readers a little. This is shown, I think, by the various suggested titles printed on page 57. But as he rejected those titles, it is plain that he thought them unsatisfactory, and that he refrained from raising in the title at least the question whether the murder of Edwin Drood was accomplished.

3. I had prepared materials for a chapter on the wrappers of Dickens's novels as used in the monthly parts, but it is not necessary to go into particulars. I am glad to find myself in full agreement with the eminent Dickens scholar, Mr. B W. Matz, who attaches no importance to the covers. I put no trust in the wrapper of *Edwin Drood* any more than I should in that of *Pickwick, Martin Chuzzlewit, Little Dorrit, Dombey and Son*, and many others, for a suggestion of any intricate points in any of their plots. The only covers which may be reliable in this respect are *A Tale of Two Cities, Oliver Twist*, and *Sketches by Boz*. Each of these works was issued in parts after their respective stories had appeared complete in other forms. All the others must have been designed before the first parts were published, and knowing the freedom which Dickens allowed himself we can attach little importance to the evidence of a particular cover as an index to the story.

When Mr. Marcus Stone, R.A., completed his seventy-second year, on 4th July 1912, he was interviewed by a representative of the *Morning Post*, and said:

> The cover of *Our Mutual Friend*, with the representation of different incidents in the story, I drew after seeing an amount of matter equivalent to no more than the first two one-shilling monthly parts. Here it is: you will see that I depicted among other characters, Mr. Silas Wegg. Well, I was aware that Wegg had a wooden leg, but I wanted to know whether this was his right or his left leg, as there was nothing in the material before me that threw light on this point. To my surprise, Dickens said: 'I do not know. I do not think I had identified the leg.' That was the only time I ever knew him to be at fault on a point of this kind, for as a rule he was ready to describe down to the minutest details the personal characteristics, and, I might almost add, the life-history of the creations of his fancy.

4. But the final proof of the impossibility of making trustworthy deductions from the cover is to be found in the fact that no readers read it in the same way. In proof of this I give the readings of Professor Henry Jackson, Mr. Andrew Lang, Dr. M. R. James, and Mr. Cuming Walters. Through the great kindness of Mr. Hugh Thomson the artist, who has made a study of this subject and has given me his results, I am able to add another interpretation certainly of no lower authority than those which accompany it.

PROFESSOR JACKSON'S READING

> We may fairly presume that the figures in the four corners represent comedy, tragedy, the opium-woman, and the Chinaman. In the nave of the Cathedral, Edwin and Rosa pair off against Jasper and Crisparkle. Despite the discrepancy which Mr. Lang points out, I think that the lower of the two pictures on our left shows Jasper and Rosa in the garden of the Nuns' House. In the upper side-piece, the girl is, I am sure, Rosa flying from Jasper's pursuit, in full view of a placard announcing Edwin's disappearance. It is true that the hatless girl with her hair streaming down her back does not answer very well to Dickens's description of Rosa, and has no resemblance to Sir L. Fildes's pictures of her: but if Dickens, when he had not yet thought out his conception of her personality, told Collins to draw a frightened girl of seventeen running away from school, no more than this could be expected. For the scheme of the sketch, compare the picture in *Bleak House*, which shows Lady Dedlock, as she mounts the staircase, turning to look at a bill announcing a reward for the discovery of the murderer of Tulkinghorn. That placards and advertisements, imploring Edwin to communicate with his uncle, had been widely circulated, we have been told at p. 182. On the right, the two men in the lower picture are, I suppose, Jasper and Durdles ascending the tower on the night of 'the unaccountable expedition'; while the man above is Jasper on Christmas Eve looking down at '*that*,' p. 276: 'Look down, look down! You see what lies at the bottom there?' p. 274. I demur to Mr. Lang's statements that the young man whom I venture to identify with Jasper is represented as 'whiskerless,' and that the figure which I take to be Durdles is well-dressed.

Professor Jackson then mentions the views of Mr. Proctor and Mr. Lang on the important vignette at the bottom of the page:

> For my own part, I suspect that the upright figure represents Drood, but that the Drood which it represents is a phantom of Jasper's imagination. Let us suppose that an advertisement for a ring known to have been in the possession of the late Edwin Drood appears in the local newspaper, and that Jasper, now for the first time aware of the ring's existence, goes to the crypt to look for it.

Dickens might well suppose him at such a moment to see a vision of the murdered man, and might instruct Collins to represent what Jasper imagined himself to see. Indeed, I fancy that I recognise an intentional contrast between the two figures: the one in the foreground, full of movement, solidly drawn; the other, in the background, statuesque, and a little shadowy. Doubtless Dickens was anxious that the reader should not know too much; and if he made Collins give visible form to a hallucination of Jasper's brain, I for one do not think the procedure illegitimate. It is sad that Dickens did not live to explain the innocent deception which, as I imagine, he meant for a few months to practise upon his readers.

MR. ANDREW LANG'S INTERPRETATION IN 'THE PUZZLE OF DICKENS'S LAST PLOT'

The cover lies before the reader. In the left-hand top corner appears an allegorical female figure of joy, with flowers. The central top space contains the front of Cloisterham Cathedral, or rather, the nave. To the left walks Edwin, with hyacinthine locks, and a thoroughly classical type of face, and Grecian nose. *Like Datchery, he does not wear, but carries his hat*; this means nothing, if they are in the nave. He seems bored. On his arm is Rosa; *she* seems bored; she trails her parasol, and looks away from Edwin, looks down, to her right. On the spectator's right march the surpliced men and boys of the choir. Behind them is Jasper, black whiskers and all; he stares after Edwin and Rosa; his right hand hides his mouth. In the corner above him is an allegorical female, clasping a stiletto.

Beneath Edwin and Rosa is, first, an allegorical female figure, looking at a placard, headed 'LOST,' on a door. Under that again, is a girl in a garden-chair; a young man, whiskerless, with wavy hair, kneels and kisses her hand. She looks rather unimpassioned. I conceive the man to be Landless, taking leave of Rosa after urging his hopeless suit for which Helena, we learn, 'seems to compassionate him.' He has avowed his passion, early in the story, to Crisparkle. Below, the opium hag is smoking. On the other side, under the figures of Jasper and the choir, the young man who kneels to the girl is seen bounding up a spiral staircase. His left hand is on the iron railing; he stoops over it, looking down at others who follow him. His right hand, the index finger protruded, points upward, and, by chance or design, points straight at Jasper in the vignette above. Beneath this man (clearly Landless) follows a tall man in a 'bowler' hat, a 'cut-away' coat, and trousers which show an inch of white stocking above the low shoes. His profile is hid by the wall of the spiral staircase: he might be Grewgious of the shoes, white stockings, and short trousers, but he may be Tartar: he takes two steps at a stride. Beneath him a youngish man, in a low, soft, clerical hat and a black pea-coat, ascends, looking downwards and backwards. This is clearly Crisparkle. A Chinaman is smoking opium beneath.

In the central lowest space, a dark and whiskered man enters a dark chamber; his left hand is on the lock of the door; in his right he holds up a lantern. The light of the lantern reveals a young man in a soft hat of Tyrolese shape. His features are purely classical, his nose is Grecian, his locks are long (at least, according to the taste of to-day); he wears a light paletot, buttoned to the throat; his right arm hangs by his side; his left hand is thrust into the breast of his coat. He calmly regards the dark man with the lantern. That man, of course, is Jasper. The young man is EDWIN DROOD, of the Grecian nose, hyacinthine locks, and classic features, as in Sir L. Fildes's third illustration.

Mr. Proctor correctly understood the unmistakable meaning of this last design, Jasper entering the vault:

'To-day the dead are living,
The lost is found to-day.'

DR. JAMES'S VIEW

In the *Cambridge Review* for 9th March 1911 Dr. James says:

Now, as to the figures at the angles and the scene at the top there is general agreement. As to those on the left, H. J. is, I think, right in calling the upper one Rosa's flight; but the lower one *cannot* be Jasper and Rosa. The young man has a moustache. Jasper had none, and has none in the two pictures of him on this same cover. Also, the artist has carefully emphasised the fact that the girl is indifferent to her suitor. The figures, I believe, represent Rosa and Neville Landless.

On the right, H. J. assumes that there are two scenes. I am clear that there is but one: for, whereas, on the left side the two scenes are separated by a sprig of the rose-wreath which surrounds the centre, and a similar sprig parts them from the top scene, there is on the right only the division from the top scene, managed in the same way as on the left. And yet, had the scene been two, there was great necessity to separate them, inasmuch as they are taking place in the same surroundings, namely, the winding staircase. As to the identity of the three men, the lowest one is a cleric, Crisparkle, the next above him I will not identify; the uppermost is either Jasper or just possibly (since he is pointing pretty directly at the figure of Jasper in the top scene, and seems to be acting as a guide to those below him) Datchery.

Dr. James dissents from Dr. Jackson as to the central vignette at the bottom. No phantom of the imagination is there. We have a real person, as is shown by the fact that he casts a shadow on the wall behind him.

MR. HUGH THOMSON'S READING

Mr. Hugh Thomson wrote the following notes on 3rd April 1912, and they are now printed for the first time:

> But to get to the cover to which you particularly directed my attention. It was designed, I take it, primarily as a decoration, and not as a series of representations of the characters to appear in the book. Consequently, there is but little definite character-drawing in any of the groups with the exception of the one at the bottom of the page, where Jasper is depicted exactly as I should wish him depicted, dark and saturnine 'with thick, lustrous black hair and whiskers.' If the other figure is merely a wraith conjured up by Jasper's evil opium-soaked conscience, it is as substantial as one of the ghosts of Hamlet's father given to us on the stage time after time without protest. But in a black and white design for a popular serial it is scarcely possible to be subtle, and at the same time plainly intelligible. So it may be a ghost, or it may be Edwin in the flesh, or Neville Landless got up to represent Edwin. It is a very effective little cut. In the other groups, Jasper is not so unmistakable, but, of course, in the upper

drawings the sleek, clerical-looking personage with his hand at his mouth is meant to represent Jasper. The staircase groups, I can't identify. The young men in both may be meant to represent Jasper. They are not in the least like that sombre personage, but just colourless young men. In the garden scene one cannot think that the kneeling figure pressing the girl's fingers to his lips is meant for Jasper at all. It has a mop of fair hair and boasts a moustache, and in the scene in the garden of the Nuns' House Rosa did not permit Jasper to approach her so nearly. In the picture there is no suggestion of the repugnance and fear with which she regarded Jasper. Don't you think it reasonable to suggest that this little picture illustrates a scene to take place much later in the book, a scene Dickens did not live to write? It might be Edwin Drood returned from abroad or from disguise. Edwin Drood making love to Helena Landless. In chapter viii. he was 'already enough impressed by Helena to feel indignant that Helena's brother should dispose of him (Edwin) so coolly' to Rosebud.

Or could it be Tartar proposing to Rosebud? But Tartar had no moustache either as himself or as Datchery, and the girl's figure has a suggestion of lithe dignity which I don't associate with the 'little beauty' Rosebud.

I agree with the author of *About Edwin Drood* that Edwin was not worth while bringing back, but it is possible that he was to return, and that this is he in the garden scene. In the space above this the female figure scanning a placard 'LOST' is, I think, merely allegorical, and not meant to represent Rosebud fleeing from Jasper. In the book she leaves Cloisterham so neat and pretty that Joe, the omnibus man, would have liked to keep for himself the love she sent to Miss Twinkleton.

MR. CUMING WALTERS'S READING

There is another view to which I strongly incline, first stated by Mr. Cuming Walters. I take the erect figure in the bottom vignette to be Datchery. It is not Edwin. The large hat and the tightish surtout are the articles of clothing on which Dickens lays stress in his description of Datchery. Mr. Lang says that the figure is that of a young man in a longish loose greatcoat, not a tightish surtout such as Datchery wore, but I agree with Mr. Cuming Walters that the figure corresponds with the description of Datchery. Edwin as seen above with Rosa in the cathedral is not wearing a coat of this sort. His hat also is different. On examining the figure Mr. H. B. Irving said to me: 'That looks uncommonly like a woman in disguise.'

None of us has a right to dogmatise, but the variety of opinions among those who have studied the cover shows that no certain conclusion can be drawn from the illustrations. The arguments advanced previously tend to make this practically certain. In the discussion of the problem a wholly disproportionate weight has been laid on the illustrated cover. It would hardly bear that weight even if every one were agreed as to the reading of the pictures, and there is no such agreement.

CHAPTER IV—THE METHODS OF DICKENS

HALF-WAY IN DICKENS

Dickens has left us one-half of his last story. It was to be completed in twelve parts, and six parts were published. We can only infer and guess at the way in which the author would have completed it. Would he have brought many new characters on the stage, or are we to believe that the main characters are already there, and that it is through the revealing of their secrets that the end is to be reached? To give a positive reply is impossible, and yet we may learn something of Dickens's methods by studying his complete books. Supposing we had only one-half of each book in our possession, might we expect that the complete story would introduce us to many fresh characters? I give the results of some investigations from the later novels.

THE LENGTH OF DICKENS'S NOVELS

Edwin Drood, as we have it, runs in round numbers to about 100,000 words. When completed it would have been 200,000 words. This would have made it slightly longer than *Great Expectations*, which may be estimated at 160,000 words. *A Tale of Two Cities* runs to 143,000 words. *Edwin Drood*, while slightly longer than this, would have been very much shorter than the larger works of Dickens. *David Copperfield* has about 306,000 words; *Bleak House*, 308,000, and *Our Mutual Friend*, 297,000. All these are practically the same length. *Barnaby Rudge* has about 264,000 words.

'BLEAK HOUSE'

I begin with *Bleak House*, which is one of the latest and most elaborate of Dickens's stories. In the first half the characters arrive in crowds. I make out in the first chapter ten or eleven. The second chapter brings My Lady Dedlock, Sir Leicester Dedlock, Mr. Tulkinghorn, and others. The third brings Esther Summerson and John Jarndyce, besides half a dozen more. The fourth brings us the Jellybys, with Mr. Guppy, and others. Krook and Nemo are the fresh arrivals in chapter v.; Mr. Harold Skim-pole arrives in chapter vi., with the Coavinses. In chapter vii. I make out six arrivals at least. Chapter viii. gives us the Pardiggles, Mr. Gusher, the brickmaker, and family, and Jenny, his wife. In chapter ix. Mr. Lawrence Boythorn arrives alone; chapter x. gives us the Snagsbys, their predecessor, Peffer, the two prentices, and Guster, the servant. Miss Flite comes with chapter xi., and along with her appear the young surgeon, the beadle, Mrs. Perkins, Mrs. Anastasia Piper, and a few more. Chapter xii. brings Mlle. Hortense, maid to Lady Dedlock, Lord Boodle and his retinue, the Right Hon. William Buffy, M.P., and his retinue. In Chapter xiii. we have Mr. Bayham Badger, Mrs. Badger, and the former husbands of Mrs. Badger are recalled. Chapter xiv. brings Mr. Turveydrop and his son, also Allan Woodcourt, the young surgeon, and we have mentioned the 'old lady with a censorious countenance,' and the late Mrs. Turveydrop. In chapter xv. we have Mrs. Blinder and the Neckett family; chapter xvii., Mrs. Woodcourt, mother of Allan; chapter xix., Mr. and Mrs. Chadband; chapter xx., Young Smallweed and Jobling, *alias* Weevle; in chapter xxi., the Grandfather and Grandmother Smallweed, Judith Smallweed, Mr. George, trooper (Uncle George, chapter vii.), and Phil Squod of the Shooting Gallery. The great Mr. Bucket appears in chapter xxii. Captain Hawdon is in chapter xxvi. In chapter xxvii. we have the Bagnet family of five. In chapter xxviii. there comes Volumnia Dedlock; Miss Wisk in chapter xxx., and Liz in chapter XXXI.

We have now reached the end of the first half, and the arrivals after that are few and unimportant. In chapter xxxii. no new character is brought on the stage, though there is talk about the noted siren, who assists at the Harmonic Meetings, and is announced as Miss M. Melvilleson, though she has been married a year and a half. In chapter xxxiii. it is mentioned that the 'Sols Arms,' a well-conducted tavern, is licensed to a highly respectable landlord, Mr. J. G. Bogsby. After that we have no new character till chapter xxxvii., where we are introduced to Mr. W. Grubble, the landlord of that very clean little tavern, 'The Dedlock Arms.' Vholes is introduced by Skimpole as the man who gives him something and called it commission. Mr. Vholes has the privilege of supporting an aged father in the Vale of Taunton, and has a red eruption here and there upon his face. He has three daughters—Emma, Jane, and Caroline—and cannot afford to be selfish. In chapter xxxviii. we meet Mrs. Guppy, 'an old lady in a large cap, with rather a red nose, and rather an unsteady eye, but smiling all over.' Then in chapter xl. there are the cousins of Sir Leicester Dedlock. In chapter xliii. Mrs. Skimpole and the Skimpole family are introduced, and in chapter liii. Mrs. Bucket. It will be observed that some of these can scarcely be called new characters, and that not one is of any real importance, that is, so far as *Bleak House* is concerned. Dickens in the middle of his story had practically put every actor upon the stage. The story was to be developed by the characters to whom the reader had been introduced. I have calculated that in the first half there are about one hundred and six characters of greater or less importance. In the second half there are, on the most generous computation, only sixteen, and not one of them plays a vital part in the development of the tale.

'OUR MUTUAL FRIEND'

I take next *Our Mutual Friend*, and with this I must deal more briefly. *Our Mutual Friend* is remarkable for the profusion of characters in the first half. In the second chapter there are sixteen at least, including Mr. and Mrs. Veneering, Mr. and Mrs. Podsnap, Mortimer Lightfoot, Eugene Wrayburn, and John Harmon. The Wilfers come in chapter iv.; in chapter v. Silas Wegg and the Boffins, and almost every chapter adds to the company till we get to the middle. After that there is an abrupt cessation. There are not more than half a dozen new characters named in the second part, and all of them are wholly insignificant, the Deputy Lock, Gruff and Glum, the Greenwich pensioner, the Archbishop of Greenwich, a waiter, Mrs. Sprodgkin, the exacting member of the fold, and the contractor of 500,000 power. In *Our Mutual Friend* every character of any significance has been introduced when the first half ends. The few stragglers who come later have practically no effect on the story.

'LITTLE DORRIT'

In *Little Dorrit* we have the old profuseness of characters; in the first half nearly one hundred, and in the second half there are practically no new characters at all. Mr. Tinkler, the valet to Mr. Dorrit, and Mr. Eustace, the classical tourist, can hardly be counted. In chapter xxi., 'The History of a Self-Tormentor,' we have Charlotte Dawes, the false friend, who vanishes instantly, and counts for nothing. Thus, I think, we may say, taking the three long books of Dickens's later period, that in each it was his manner to introduce no new characters of the least import in the second half of his books. But it may be worth while to glance at his practice in the shorter tales, *A Tale of Two Cities* and *Great Expectations*.

'A TALE OF TWO CITIES'

In the second half of this fine book there are practically no new characters that I can trace. The epithet can hardly be applied to the President of the trial at the Conciergerie.

'GREAT EXPECTATIONS'

It is now agreed that one of Dickens's most perfect books is *Great Expectations*. It is known also that Dickens complied with a suggestion of Lord Lytton's, which modified the plot—not seriously nor disagreeably. Here again in the second part we have very few fresh characters. We have the Colonel in Newgate introduced to Mr. Wemmick, but he is 'sure to be assassinated on Monday.' Let us not forget Miss Skiffins, a good sort of fellow, with a high regard both for Wemmick and the Aged. There is the retrospective Provis, but the characters introduced belong to the past. Finally, in chapter xlvi., we have a pleasant glimpse of the Barley family and of Mrs. Whymple, the best of housewives, and the motherly friend of Clara and Herbert. It is she who fosters and regulates with equal kindness and discretion their mutual love. 'It was understood that nothing of a tender nature could possibly be confided to Old Barley, by reason of his being totally unequal to the consideration of any subject more psychological than Gout, Rum, and Purser's Stores.'

These are all the books of which I have made a close personal examination. I believe that the general result will be the same in all save two or three exceptional works, such as *Barnaby Rudge*. Whether he consciously acted on the principle that no new characters should be introduced after half the story was told, it is impossible to say. It seems certain, however, that he acted upon it.

WILKIE COLLINS 'AHEAD OF ALL THE FIELD'

Dickens was no great reader, and it is plain by what he did not say, as well as by what he did say, that he did not on the whole admire ardently the work of his contemporaries. But he made a special exception in the case of Wilkie Collins, with whom he collaborated on more than one occasion, as in the story *No Thoroughfare*. He published in his own magazine some of Collins's best detective stories, including *The Woman in White*, *No Name*, and *The Moonstone*. Of these stories Dickens put first *No Name*. *The Moonstone* he criticised in one of his letters to Wills. At first he thought it in many respects 'much better than anything he has done,' but afterwards he wrote, 26th July 1868: 'I quite agree with you about *The Moonstone*. The construction is wearisome beyond endurance, and there is a vein of obstinate conceit in it that makes enemies of readers.' [90]

In September 1862 he wrote in enthusiastic terms of admiration about *No Name*. This I take to be a very weighty and significant letter, as will appear in the sequel:

> I have gone through the second volume [*No Name*] at a sitting, and I find it *wonderfully fine*. It goes on with an ever-rising power and force in it that fills me with admiration. It is as far before and beyond *The Woman in White* as that was beyond the wretched common level of fiction-writing. There are some touches in the Captain which no one but a born (and cultivated) writer could get near— could draw within hail of. And the originality of Mrs. Wragge, without compromise of her probability, involves a really great achievement. But they are all admirable; Mr. Noel Vanstone and the housekeeper, both in their way as meritorious as the rest; Magdalen wrought out with truth, energy, sentiment, and passion, of the very first water.

> I cannot tell you with what a strange dash of pride as well as pleasure I read the great results of your hard work. Because, as you know, I was certain from the Basil days that you were the Writer who would come ahead of all the Field—being the only one who combined invention and power, both humorous and pathetic, with that invincible determination to work, and that profound conviction that nothing of worth is to be done without work, of which triflers and feigners have no conception. [91]

Mr. Swinburne in his study of Wilkie Collins writes:

> It is apparently the general opinion—an opinion which seems to me incontestable—that no third book of their author's can be ranked as equal with *The Woman in White* and *The Moonstone*: two works of not more indisputable than incomparable ability. *No Name* is an only less excellent example of as curious and original a talent. [92a]

This was not the opinion of Dickens.

'A BACKWARD LIGHT'

On 6th October 1859 Dickens replied to a suggestion by Collins on the working out of *A Tale of Two Cities*. The italics are mine:

> I do not positively say that the point you put might not have been done in your manner; but I have a very strong conviction that it would have been overdone in that manner—too elaborately trapped, baited, and prepared—in the main anticipated, and its interest wasted. This is quite apart from the peculiarity of the Doctor's [Dr. Manette—*A Tale of Two Cities*] character, as affected by his imprisonment; which of itself would, to my thinking, render it quite out of the question to put the reader inside of him before the proper time, in respect of matters that were dim to himself through being, in a diseased way, morbidly shunned by him. *I think the business of art is to lay all that ground carefully, not with the care that conceals itself—to show, by a backward light, what everything has been working to,—but only to suggest, until the fulfilment comes. These are the ways of Providence, of which ways all art is but a little imitation.* [92b]

EDGAR ALLAN POE AND DICKENS: A MYSTIFICATION

Could Dickens keep his secrets well? In other words, could he prevent his readers from fathoming a mystery till the proper moment of the *dénouement?* An important help to the answering of this question will be found in the essay on Charles Dickens by Edgar Allan Poe, who was a critic of extraordinary penetration. If any one could detect a secret it was he. But he was also much given to mystification, and it is not wise to accept anything he says without verifying it. The essay on Dickens turns largely on *Barnaby Rudge*, and, to the best of my belief, it has not been strictly examined.

POE'S CLAIM

Poe says:

> We are not prepared to say, so positively as we could wish, whether by the public at large, the whole *mystery* of the murder committed by Rudge, with the identity of the Maypole ruffian with Rudge himself, was fathomed at any period previous to the period intended, or, if so, whether at a period so early as materially to interfere with the interest designed; but we are forced, through sheer modesty, to suppose this the case; since, by ourselves individually, the secret was distinctly understood immediately upon the perusal of the story of Solomon Daisy, which occurs at the seventh page of this volume of three hundred and twenty-three. In the number of the Philadelphia *Saturday Evening Post* for 1st May 1841 (the tale having then only begun), will be found a prospective notice of some length, in which we make use of the following words:

> 'That Barnaby is the son of the murderer may not appear evident to our readers—but we will explain. The person murdered is Mr. Reuben Haredale. He was found assassinated in his bed-chamber. His steward (Mr. Rudge, senior) and his gardener (name not mentioned) are missing. At first both are suspected. "Some months afterward"—here we use the words of the story—"the steward's body, scarcely to be recognised but by his clothes and the watch and ring he wore, was found at the bottom of a piece of water in the grounds, with a deep gash in the breast, where he had been stabbed by a knife. He was only partly dressed; and all the people agreed that he had been sitting up reading in his own room, where there were many traces of blood, and was suddenly fallen upon and killed, before his master."

'Now, be it observed, it is not the author himself who asserts that the steward's body was found; he has put the words in the mouth of one of his characters. His design is to make it appear, in the *dénouement*, that the steward, Rudge, first murdered the gardener, then went to his master's chamber, murdered *him*, was interrupted by his (Rudge's) wife, whom he seized and held *by the wrist*, to prevent her giving the alarm—that he then, after possessing himself of the booty desired, returned to the gardener's room, exchanged clothes with him, put upon the corpse his own watch and ring, and secreted it where it was afterwards discovered at so late a period that the features could not be identified.'

This is the prediction we have to examine. In the first place, was such an article published in the Philadelphia *Saturday Evening Post* for 1st May 1841? Mr. J. H. Ingram, the chief authority on Poe in this country, very kindly informs me that this review has never been reprinted in any edition of Poe's works. Should it not be searched out and reprinted in full? I should like to see the context of Poe's extract, and I should like still more to be sure that the article appeared as he says it did. Mr. Ingram has no doubt that the article appeared as stated by Poe. Mr. J. H. Whitty of Richmond, Va., kindly informs me that all the early files of the *Post* are inaccessible.

In the second place, Poe affirms that the article appeared in the Philadelphia paper for 1st May 1841, and that the tale was only then begun. As for that, *Barnaby Rudge* was first published as a volume in 1841, after having run as a serial in the pages of *Master Humphrey's Clock* from 13th February 1841 to 27th November 1841. I have failed to find the precise date of its first appearance in America. No doubt it appeared in serial form, and the first instalments on which Poe bases his assertions should have been printed in America considerably earlier than 1st May. But the assertion which chiefly demands scrutiny is very definitely made by Poe. He says: The secret was *distinctly* understood *immediately* upon the perusal of the story of Solomon Daisy.' The italics are mine.

THE STORY OF SOLOMON DAISY

We turn to the story of Solomon Daisy 'as told in the *Maypole* at any time for four and twenty years.' It is very simple and matter-of-fact. It tells how Mr. Reuben Haredale, of The Warren, a widower with one child, left the place when his lady died. He went up to London, where he stopped some months, but, finding that place as lonely as The Warren, he suddenly came back with his little girl, bringing with him besides, that day, only two women servants, and his steward and a gardener. The rest stayed behind in

London, and were to follow next day. That night, an old gentleman who lived at Chigwell Row, and had long been poorly, died, and an order came to Solomon at half after twelve o'clock at night to go and toll the passing bell. Solomon relates to a thrilled audience how he went out in a windy, rainy, very dark night; how he entered the church, trimmed the candle, thought of old tales about dead people rising and sitting at the head of their own graves, fancying that he saw the old gentleman who was just dead, wrapping his shroud round him, and shivering as if he felt it cold. At length he started up and took the bell rope in his hands. At that minute there rang—not that bell, for he had scarcely touched the rope—but another! It was only for an instant, and even then the wind carried the sound away, but he heard it. He listened for a long time, but it rang no more. He then tolled his own bell and ran home to bed as fast as he could touch the ground. Next morning came the news that Mr. Reuben Haredale was found murdered in his bed-chamber, and in his hand was a piece of the cord attached to an alarm bell outside, which hung in his room, and had been cut asunder, no doubt by the murderer when he seized it. 'That was the bell I heard.' He further relates how the steward and the gardener were both missing, both suspected, but never found. The body of Mr. Rudge, the steward—scarcely to be recognised by his clothes and the watch and the ring he wore—was found months afterwards at the bottom of a piece of water in the grounds with a deep gash in the breast where he had been stabbed by a knife. Every one knew now that the gardener must be the murderer, and Solomon Daisy predicted that he would be heard of. That is the whole story as told by Solomon Daisy, and Poe affirms that he perceived from this story: (1) That the steward Rudge first murdered the gardener; (2) that he then went to his master's chamber and murdered him; (3) that he was interrupted by Rudge's wife, whom he seized and held by the wrist to prevent her giving the alarm; (4) that he possessed himself of the booty, returned to the gardener's room, exchanged clothes with him, put upon the corpse his own watch and ring, and secreted it where it was afterwards discovered at so late a period that the features could not be identified.

WHERE POE FAILED

Poe admits that his preconceived ideas were not entirely correct:

> The gardener was murdered, not before, but after his master; and that Rudge's wife seized *him* by the wrist, instead of his seizing *her*, has so much the air of a mistake on the part of Mr. Dickens that we can scarcely speak of our own version as erroneous. The grasp of a murderer's bloody hand on the wrist of a woman *enceinte* would have been more likely to produce the effect described (and this

every one will allow) than the grasp of the hand of the woman upon the wrist of the assassin. We may, therefore, say of our supposition, as Talleyrand said of some cockney's bad French—*que s'il ne soit pas Français assurément donc il le doit être*—that if we did not rightly prophesy, yet, at least, our prophecy should have been right.

I have no hesitation in saying that this is largely a piece of pure mystification, another *Tale of the Grotesque and Arabesque*. It is conceivable that Poe guesses from Solomon Daisy's story that the steward Rudge murdered the gardener and his master. It follows that the steward changed clothes with the murdered gardener, put upon the corpse his own watch and ring, and secreted it where it was afterwards discovered at so late a period that the features could not be identified. But that Poe should have guessed immediately after reading Solomon Daisy's story that he seized and held by the wrist his wife to prevent her giving the alarm is beyond belief. 'By the wrist' are the three significant words, and they prove that Poe must have had before him when writing the parts of the novel up to and including chapter V. For it is in the fifth chapter that the first mention is made of the smear of blood on Barnaby's wrist. We read there:

> They who knew the Maypole story, and could remember what the widow was, before her husband's and his master's murder, understood it well. They recollected how the change had come, and could call to mind that when her son was born, upon the very day the deed was known, he bore upon his wrist what seemed a smear of blood but half washed out.

Near the beginning of chapter lxii., where Rudge is making his confession in prison, he says of his wife:

> Did I see her fall upon the ground; and, when I stooped to raise her, did she thrust me back with a force that cast me off as if I had been a child, staining the hand with which she clasped my wrist? Is *that* fancy?

To claim that the seizing of the wrist could have been deduced from Solomon Daisy's story by itself is to affirm an impossibility.

And so vanishes the main value of the prediction. If Poe wrote that article in the *Saturday Evening Post*, he wrote it after having read the fifth chapter of Dickens's novel.

WHERE POE SUCCEEDED

It may be asked whether Poe discovered anything from his reading of the first pages. The only thing which he may have guessed is the thing which it was comparatively easy to guess. He may have conjectured that the mysterious stranger at the Maypole was Rudge Redux. When this surmise had been lodged in his mind the other deductions follow as a matter of course from later chapters, as the tale unfolds itself. Even if Poe identified the stranger at the Maypole with the murderer it was no great feat, for the murderer is closely disguised, from which any intelligent reader would infer that he has a motive for fearing detection in an old haunt. He is shabbily dressed; he is very curious about the people and events at The Warren; he is suspected as a criminal of some kind by the cronies; he strikes Joe as he leaves. On the road he threatens Varden with murder. This shows us that we have before us a fugitive criminal. He is presented to us with all the marks of a villain in hiding. It may be noted that from Solomon Daisy's story the inference is that only one of two men committed the murder of Reuben Haredale, the gardener or Rudge. There has also been a difficulty in identifying the remains. This leaves Poe no special credit. There is considerable keenness in his conjecture that the treatment of the Gordon Riots was an afterthought of Dickens. Poe says:

> The title of the book, the elaborate and pointed manner of the commencement, the impressive description of The Warren, and especially of Mrs. Rudge, go far to show that Mr. Dickens has really deceived himself—that the soul of the plot, as originally conceived, was the murder of Haredale, with the subsequent discovery of the murderer in Rudge—but that this idea was afterwards abandoned, or, rather, suffered to be merged in that of the Popish riots. The result has been most unfavourable. That which, of itself, would have proved highly effective, has been rendered nearly null by its situation. In the multitudinous outrage and horror of the Rebellion, the *one* atrocity is utterly whelmed and extinguished.

But facts, as Poe admits, are against this supposition. Dickens says in his Preface:

> If the object an author has had, in writing a book, cannot be discovered from its perusal, the probability is that it is either very deep or very shallow. Hoping that mine may lie somewhere between these two extremes, I shall say very little about it, and that only in reference to one point. No account of the Gordon Riots having been to my knowledge introduced into any work of fiction, and the

> subject presenting very extraordinary and remarkable features, I was led to project this tale.

This is final. It appears from Forster's biography that Dickens desired to expose the brutalising character of laws which led to the incessant execution of men and women comparatively innocent. It is clear also that Dickens made a special study of the contemporary newspapers and annual registers. But Forster admits that the form ultimately taken by *Barnaby Rudge* had been comprised only partially within its first design, and he admits also that the interest with which the tale begins has ceased to be its interest before the close. 'What has chiefly taken the reader's fancy at the outset almost wholly disappears in the power and passion with which, in the later chapters, great riots are described. So admirable is this description, however, that it would be hard to have to surrender it even for a more perfect structure of fable.' To this I may add that the letters to the artist Cattermole on the illustrations to *Barnaby Rudge* are very valuable for the fullness and precision of their detail.

DICKENS'S WAY

That it is legitimate to draw inferences from the hints given by Dickens I should be the last to deny. His purpose was to provide hints which, when contemplated with what he called a backward glance, should appear luminous at the end of the story. Their meaning at the time might be more or less obscure, but when from the end of the book one could look back upon its course even to the beginning, he would see that the artist had a purpose all through, and that he was steadily preparing his reader for the *dénouement*. Of this I give a striking proof, on which, so far as I am aware, little stress has been laid. [104] The *Edinburgh Review* of July 1857 contains an article, 'The License of Modern Novelists,' in which the critic deals with *Little Dorrit*, and denounces his charges against the administrative system of England. Among other things, the reviewer says: 'Even the catastrophe in *Little Dorrit* is evidently borrowed from the recent fall of houses in Tottenham Court Road, which happens to have appeared in the newspapers at a convenient period.' Dickens, for the first and only time in his life, so far as I know, publicly replied to a reviewer. He wrote an article in *Household Words* of 1st August 1857, entitled 'Curious Misprint in the *Edinburgh Review*,' in which he turned upon his critic fiercely and sharply. He quotes the sentence about the catastrophe in *Little Dorrit*, and goes on to say:

> Thus, the Reviewer. The Novelist begs to ask him whether there is no License in his writing those words, and stating that assumption as a truth, when any man accustomed to the critical examination of a book cannot

fail, attentively turning over the pages of *Little Dorrit*, to observe that that catastrophe is carefully prepared for from the very first presentation of the old house in the story; that when Rigaud, the man who is crushed by the fall of the house, first enters it (hundreds of pages before the end) he is beset by a mysterious fear and shuddering; that the rotten and crazy state of the house is laboriously kept before the reader, whenever the house is shown; that the way to the demolition of the man and the house together is paved all through the book with a painful minuteness and reiterated care of preparation, the necessity of which (in order that the thread may be kept in the reader's mind through nearly two years) is one of the adverse incidents of the serial form of publication? It may be nothing to the question that Mr. Dickens now publicly declares, on his word of honour, that that catastrophe was written, was engraved on steel, was printed, had passed through the hands of compositors, readers for the press, and pressmen, and was in type and in proof in the Printing House of Messrs. Bradbury and Evans before the accident in Tottenham Court Road occurred. But, it is much to the question that an honourable reviewer might have easily traced this out in the internal evidence of the book itself, before he stated, for a fact, what is utterly and entirely, in every particular and respect, untrue.

The blows are dealt with a will, and it should be noted that Dickens is more irritated at the stupidity of the reviewer in failing to see the way in which he contrived the catastrophe than at his mistake in the fact. It is to be noted also that Dickens considered that his serial form of publication compelled him to be almost too minute, copious, and constant in keeping the thread in the mind of a reader whose attention had to be maintained for nearly two years.

PART II—ATTEMPT AT A SOLUTION

CHAPTER V—WAS EDWIN DROOD MURDERED?

I reply in the affirmative, and for the following reasons:

I.

1. The external testimonies as given in a previous chapter are all explicit as far as they go in their testimony that in the intention of Dickens Edwin Drood was murdered. There is first the testimony of John Forster. To him Dickens plainly declared that a nephew was to be murdered by his uncle. The murderer was to discover that his crime was useless for its purpose, but he was not to be convicted in the ordinary way. It was by means of a gold ring, which had resisted the corrosive effects of the lime into which the body had been cast, that the murderer and the person murdered were to be identified.

2. Madame Perugini corroborates Forster's testimony, and points out that the only thing on which he is not positive is the ending of Neville Landless. He guards himself by saying, 'I think,' and this makes his testimony to the more important facts the more impressive. Madame Perugini, who thoroughly understood the relations between Forster and Dickens, finds it impossible to believe that Dickens should have altered his plan without communicating with Forster. Forster's strong character, and the peculiar friendship that existed between him and Dickens, make it impossible to believe that Dickens should suddenly become 'underhand,' and we might say treacherous, by inventing a plot which he did not intend to carry into execution. Forster became a little jealous of Dickens's confidence, and more than a little exacting in his demands on it. This Dickens knew, and smiled at occasionally. But he was very careful not to wound his friend's very sensitive nature, and he so trusted Forster's judgment as to be uneasy and unhappy if he did not obtain its sanction for his decisions and his actions. If there had been any change of plan Forster would certainly have been told. He never was told.

3. Again, we know that Charles Dickens the younger positively declared that he heard from his father's lips that Edwin Drood was dead. I have been able to print part of a play written by Charles Dickens the younger and Joseph Hatton. This shows beyond contradiction that the authors believed Drood to be dead. Mr. Hatton says: 'Consulting his son, Charles, to whom I offered my sketch, I found that his father had revealed to him sufficient of the plot to clearly indicate how the story was to end.' How far this may apply to details we cannot be sure, but most certainly it certifies the death.

4. To this I may add that Madame Perugini's own firm belief that Drood was dead is of no small importance, considering that she was the wife of Charles Allston Collins, who drew the much discussed wrapper. It did not occur either to Madame Perugini or her husband that there was any doubt as to the fate of Edwin Drood.

5. The weighty letter of Sir Luke Fildes printed on pages 54–5 confirms unmistakably and strongly the witness already adduced. Fildes was the sole illustrator of *The Mystery of Edwin Drood*, and he testifies that Collins did not in the least know the significance of the various groups on the wrapper. Further, when Sir Luke was puzzled by the statement that John Jasper was described as wearing a neckerchief that would go twice round his neck he drew Dickens's attention to the circumstance that he had previously dressed Jasper as wearing a little black tie once round the neck, and asked why the alteration was made. Dickens, a little disconcerted, suddenly asked, 'Can you keep a secret?' He then said: 'I must have the double necktie! It is necessary, for Jasper strangles Edwin Drood with it.' Fildes was impressed by Dickens's earnestness, and resented the suggestion often made that Dickens's hints dropped to members of his family or friends may have been intentionally misleading. 'It is a little startling,' says Sir Luke, 'after more than thirty-five years of profound belief in the nobility of character and sincerity of Charles Dickens, to be told now that he probably was more or less of a humbug on such occasions.'

I cannot but feel that the external testimony is too strong to be explained away, and it ought to be read and pondered in its entirety.

II. DICKENS'S OWN NOTE

In the Memoranda made by Dickens for chapter xii., and printed on page 63, we read that Jasper 'lays the ground for the manner of the murder, to come out at last. Night picture of the Cathedral.' Mr. Lang himself admits, 'It seems almost undeniable that, when Dickens wrote this note, he meant Jasper to succeed in murdering Edwin.' [113]

III. THE ADMITTED TESTIMONY OF THE BOOK

The proof that Edwin Drood was murdered is to my mind mainly to be found in the pages of the story. One would have to print a large part of it in order to convey the impressive and unmistakable force of the whole, but perhaps it is better to read it as Dickens wrote it. For he himself advances nothing to modify or mitigate the conclusion that, as the result of a carefully designed plot, Edwin Drood was foully murdered by his uncle. Happily it is not necessary to spend much space on this. I believe that Dr. Jackson is fully justified in his statement that all who have written on the subject acknowledge that Jasper tried to murder his nephew, and believed himself to have succeeded. We all see that Jasper had either strangled Edwin with a black scarf and committed his body to a heap of quicklime that lay about convenient, or thought that he had done so. 'We all see that the crime is to be proved by a gold ring of rubies and diamonds which Edwin has concealed about his person, though Jasper does not know it.' Mr. Proctor writes:

> It is clear that Dickens has intended to convey the impression that Edwin Drood is murdered, his body and clothes consumed, Jasper having first taken his watch and chain and shirt-pin, which cannot have been thrown into the river till the night of Christmas Day, since the watch, wound up at twenty minutes past two on Christmas Eve, had run down when found in the river.

Having arrived at this point we may proceed.

Is it conceivable that Jasper, believing himself to have succeeded in murdering his nephew, could have failed? Jasper is meant by Dickens to be a man wholly without conscience and heart. Such characters are not numerous in Dickens's books, but we have evidence that he knew them and had pondered over them. I may quote his words in *Hunted Down*:

> There is no greater mistake than to suppose that a man who is a calculating criminal, is, in any phase of his guilt otherwise than true to himself, and perfectly consistent with his whole character. Such a man commits murder, and murder is the natural culmination of his course; such a man has to outface murder, and will do it with hardihood and effrontery. It is a sort of fashion to express surprise that any notorious criminal, having such crime upon his conscience, can so brave it out. Do you think that if he had it on his conscience at all, or had a conscience to have it upon, he would ever have committed the crime? Perfectly consistent with himself, as I believe all such monsters to be, this Slinkton recovered himself, and showed a defiance that was sufficiently cold and quiet. He was white, he was haggard, he was changed; but only as a sharper who had played for a great stake and had been outwitted and had lost the game.

In *Household Words* for 14th June 1856, Dickens has an article on 'The Demeanour of Murderers.' He is referring to William Bousfield, 'the greatest villain that ever stood in the Old Bailey dock.' Bousfield's demeanour was considered exceedingly remarkable because of his composure under trial. On this Dickens says:

> Can any one, reflecting on the matter for five minutes, suppose it possible—we do not say probable, but possible—that in the breast of this poisoner there were surviving, in the days of his trial, any lingering traces of sensibility, or any wrecked fragment of the quality which we call sentiment. Can the profoundest or the simplest man alive believe that in such a heart there could have been left, by that time, any touch of pity?

The murder of Edwin Drood had been so long premeditated that Jasper had done it hundreds and thousands of times in the opium den. The motive was his fierce and wolfish passion for Rosa. He loathed his poor nephew as the chief obstacle to his wishes, and planned out in every detail a murder which would utterly remove him from the sight of men.

Jasper, then, was an unredeemed villain, but he was anything than a fool. He drugged Drood; he strangled him; he put his body in quicklime; he had time to rob the victim of his jewellery; he maintained a threatening and defiant attitude. He was not afraid that Drood would return to convict him of an attempt to murder. He had done his business. I think it worth while to point out that in Dickens's view Jasper's malevolence must have been raised to the highest point of fury on the night of the murder. For the murder was committed on a night of the wildest tempest. Trees were almost torn out of the earth, chimneys toppled into the streets, the hands of the cathedral clock were torn off, the lead from the roof was stripped away and blown into the close, and stones were displaced on the summit of the great tower. In *Barnaby Rudge* (chapter ii.) Dickens says:

> There are times when the elements being in unusual commotion, those who are bent on daring enterprises, or agitated by great thoughts, whether of good or evil, feel a mysterious sympathy with the tumult of nature, and are roused into corresponding violence. In the midst of thunder, lightning, and storm, many tremendous deeds have been committed; men, self-possessed before, have given a sudden loose to passions they could no longer control. The demons of wrath and despair have striven to emulate those who ride the whirlwind and direct the storm; and man, lashed into madness with the roaring winds and boiling waters, has become for the time as wild and merciless as the elements themselves.

IV. THE RING

As we have seen, Dickens's method is to make every hint significant, and, as a rule, not too significant. The reader at the time may fail to perceive why a particular point is mentioned, but it is not mentioned carelessly or without design. The backward glance from the end is to interpret all. Besides this there are hints in the novels to which he calls special attention, and which he thereby binds himself to redeem. Conspicuous among these in *Edwin Drood* is the sentence about the jewelled ring and betrothal over which Edwin Drood's right hand closed as it rested in its little case. He would not let Rosa's heart be grieved by those sorrowful jewels. He would restore them to the cabinet from which he had unwillingly taken them, and keep silence. He would let them be. He would let them lie unspoken of in his breast. But Dickens says: 'Among the mighty store of wonderful chains that are for ever forging, day and night, in the vast ironworks of time and circumstance, there was one chain forged in the moment of that small conclusion, riveted to the foundations of heaven and earth, and gifted with invincible force to hold and drag.' No answer to our question, no solution of the problem can be satisfactory which fails to assign its due weight to this sentence. In Proctor's first attempt at the solution of *The Mystery of Edwin Drood* contained in *Leisure Readings*, we find the following amazingly inept words: 'From the stress laid on this point, and the clear words in which its association with the mystery is spoken of, we may safely infer, I think, that it is intended partly to mislead the reader.'

Later on, Proctor, seeing the insufficiency of this, propounded another theory. This was that the attempt on Drood and his rescue were known almost immediately to Mr. Grewgious, who took possession of the ring; that when the fact that such a ring had been in Drood's pocket came to Jasper's knowledge he at once in a state of panic rushed to the vault to recover it from among the quicklime; that Drood, divining this intention, concealed himself in the vault and confronted Jasper the moment he opened the door. This theory is partly approved of by Mr. William Archer. [119] But Dickens's point is plainly that the ring was the only jewellery possessed by Drood about which Jasper knew nothing. It is the finding of the ring in the tomb that is to bring the guilt of the murder home.

As for the numerous assumptions made by Proctor, it can only be said that they have no foundation in the facts. There is no reason to believe that the attempt on Drood and his rescue were known almost immediately to Mr. Grewgious. There is no evidence that Grewgious took possession of the ring. There is no evidence that Jasper came to know that such had been in Drood's pocket. All these theories are not only without foundation, but, I think, also in plain contradiction to the whole tenor of the story.

If Drood was half dead how did he get away? According to Mr. Proctor's ingenious theory he was rescued from the bed of quicklime by Durdles. He was rescued with the skin burnt off his face, and his eyebrows gone, so that he could afterwards disguise himself as Datchery. If this is so, the quicklime must have behaved itself in a singularly obliging and accommodating manner. But, as a matter of fact, there is no evidence whatever for the theory, and the whole drift of the story makes against it. The difficulties are admitted even by those who incline to support Proctor's view and to maintain that Edwin is not dead.

Mr. Lang admits that Proctor's theory of the murder is thin, and that 'all this set of conjectures is crude to the last degree.' I am content to leave it at that. Mr. Lang has conjectures of his own. He conjectures that Mr. Grewgious visited the tomb of his lost love, Rosa's mother, and consecrated to her 'a night of memories and sighs.' He says: 'Mrs. Bud, his lost love, we have been told, was buried hard by the Sapsea monument.' This is not told by Dickens. It is better to stick by the narrative.

Supposing that Edwin was not dead, what was the meaning of the long silence? Why did he allow Neville to rest under a cloud of suspicion, and exposed to great peril? Why did he allow Jasper's persecution of Rosa? Why did he allow Helena Landless, whom he had begun more or less to love, to suffer with the rest? Are we to suppose that he came back disguised to fix the guilt on his uncle? Can we believe that he did not know that his uncle had tried to murder him? If not, are we to believe that he suspected his uncle and was not sure, and came down to try to surprise his uncle's secret and to punish him? He could only have punished him at most for an attempt at murder. Even that might have been hard to bring home, supposing he himself was not clear as to the facts. 'Fancy can suggest no reason,' writes Mr. Lang, 'why Edwin Drood, if he escaped from his wicked uncle, should go spying about instead of coming openly forward. No plausible, unfantastic reason could be invented.'

Dr. M. R. James, one of the few who still think that Edwin might not have been murdered, says in his last writing on the subject: 'I freely confess that the view that Edwin is dead solves many difficulties. A wholly satisfactory theory of the manner of his escape has never been devised; his failure to clear Neville from suspicion is hard to explain.' Mr. Lang, in what has unhappily proved his last article on the subject, in *Blackwood* for May 1911, explains that while he believed in 1905 that Jasper failed in his attempt to murder, 'now I have no theory as to how the novel would have been built up.'

V.

Those who more or less strongly still believe that Dickens meant to spare Edwin rest their case mainly on a subjective impression. Says Dr. James: 'On the other hand, whether the result would be a piece of "bad art" or not, I do think it is more in Dickens's manner to spare Edwin than to kill him. The subjective impression that he is not doomed is too strong for me to dismiss.' [122] It is difficult to argue against a subjective impression. The fact remains that Edwin Drood becomes superfluous. He has effected no lodgment in any human heart. Mr. Walters says that Drood is little more than a name-label attached to a body, a man who never excites sympathy, and whose fate causes no emotion. Proctor, who believes that Edwin Drood survived, admits that he lived unpaired. 'Rosa was to give her hand to Tartar, Helena Landless to Crisparkle, while Edwin and Mr. Grewgious were to look on approvingly, though Edwin a little sadly.'

Mr. Lang in the Gadshill edition of Dickens wrote: 'Edwin and Neville are quarrelsome cubs, not come to discretion, and the fatuity of Edwin, though not exaggerated much, makes him extremely unsympathetic.' But in his book on the subject Mr. Lang changes his view and writes: 'On re-reading the novel I find that Dickens makes Drood as sympathetic as he can.' Thus impressions alter. Gillan Vase, in her continuation of the story would make us believe that on Edwin's reappearance Rosa transferred her heart from Tartar to her old lover! But taking the story as it stands, we see that the sorrow for his death is not deep, and that no heart is broken by his disappearance. Rosa is consoled, and more than consoled. Helena grieves for her brother, and flings a shield over Rosa. Neville and Edwin have never been good friends. Grewgious has cheerfully acquiesced in, if he has not instigated, the breaking of the engagement between Rosa and Edwin. The appropriate explanation is: 'Poor youth! Poor youth!' That is all.

It has been suggested that there is a parallel between *No Thoroughfare* and *Edwin Drood*. According to Proctor it is suggested clearly in *No Thoroughfare* that Vendale has been murdered beyond all seeming hope. Proctor's real argument seems to be that Vendale is not marked for death, and does not die, and that Edwin Drood belongs to the same class. He says that Nell and Paul, Richard Carson and the other characters who die in Dickens's stories are marked for death from the beginning, but that there is not one note of death in all that Edwin does or says. I believe that this is entirely contrary to the facts. There are some who like Edwin, but none who love him. He is hated by his uncle, and hated perhaps by Neville.

In *No Thoroughfare*, a story written by Wilkie Collins and Dickens in 1867 as a Christmas Number, we have the story of a man supposed dead coming to life again. It may be noted that the only portions of this story furnished exclusively by Dickens were the overture and the third act. Collins contributed to the first and fourth act, and wrote the whole of the second. Vendale, a wine-merchant, is in love with a Swiss girl, Marguerite. She returns his affection, but her guardian Obenreizer is bitterly opposed. He consents, however, to the marriage if Vendale can double his income and make it £3000 a year. Vendale discovers that a forgery has been committed, through which £500 are missing. He is asked by the Swiss firm with which he deals to send a trustworthy messenger to investigate the fraud and discover its perpetrator. Vendale resolves to go himself, and tells Obenreizer. Obenreizer is the culprit, though Vendale does not suspect it, and the two go to Switzerland together. Obenreizer keeps planning a murder, and contrives to give Vendale an opium draught. He drugs him again, and in the course of a perilous mountain journey Vendale is roused to the knowledge that Obenreizer had set upon him, and that they were struggling desperately in the snow. Vendale rolls himself over into a gulf. But help is near. Marguerite's fears have been excited, and she has followed her lover on the journey. She engages a rescue expedition, and they find the lost man insensible. He is delirious and quite unconscious where he is. Then he seems to sink in the deadly cold, and his heart no longer beats. 'She broke from them all, and sank over him on his litter with both her living hands upon the heart that stood still.' But by and by, when the crisis of the exposure comes, 'supported on Marguerite's arm—his sunburnt colour gone, his right arm bandaged and slung over his breast—Vendale stood before the murderer a man risen from the dead.' I cannot see that this is a great surprise. Vendale was not marked for death. I think the unsophisticated reader, knowing how he is loved and how he is waited for, and how unconsciousness may pass into consciousness, would fully expect him to live. When he comes to life, he is supported on Marguerite's arm. There was no arm on which Edwin Drood could lean. Dickens can provide for his old bachelors like Newman Noggs, but he had no provision for Edwin.

THE ARGUMENTS FOR THE DISAPPEARANCE THEORY

From the Wrapper.—I am convinced after a careful perusal of nearly all that has been written on the subject that the real strength of the disappearance theory is to be found in the bottom picture of the wrapper. When Madame Perugini published the article from which I have quoted, Mr. Lang in a letter to the *Times* [127] rested his whole case on the cover design. He said:

> The chief difficulty in accepting the fact has always been that, in designs on the covers, by Mr. C. A. Collins, first husband of Mrs. Perugini, we see a young man, who is undeniably Edwin Drood, confronting Jasper in a dark vault, in the full light of a lantern held up by Jasper. Mrs. Perugini says that this figure may be regarded as 'the ghost of Edwin as seen by Jasper in his half-dazed and drugged condition,' or Helena Landless 'dressed as Datchery.' The figure is not dressed as Datchery, nor was Miss Landless fair like Drood, but very dark. As for the ghost, he is as substantial as Jasper, and it is most improbable that Dickens would have a mere hallucination designed in such

a substantial fashion, 'massive and concrete,' as Pip said of Mr. Wopsle's rendering of the part of Hamlet.

Mr. Lang in his final *Blackwood* paper repeats the assertion with unhesitating confidence. He goes so far as to say:

> Last, Dickens had instructed his son-in-law, Charles Collins (brother of Wilkie Collins), to design a pictorial cover of the numbers, in which Jasper, entering a dark vault with a lantern, finds a substantial shadow-casting Drood 'in his habit as he lived,'—soft conical hat and all,—confronting him.

As to this we note:

1. That Collins received no such instructions.

2. That neither Collins nor Luke Fildes nor any of the Dickens family read the illustration in that sense. They all supposed Edwin to be dead.

3. We also note that, in spite of Mr. Lang's confident assertions, there is no unanimity as to the meaning of the design. It may be Drood; it may be, as I think it is, Datchery; it may be Neville Landless, as Mr. Hugh Thomson has suggested. But no one is entitled to dogmatise on the subject.

4. As I have already pointed out, in the great majority of the wrappers the designs are vague and general, and cannot be verified in the narrative.

5. But to my mind the most conclusive proof that the wrapper is not to be rigidly and pedantically interpreted is that Dickens himself was the very last man in the world to give away his secrets on the cover. On this Madame Perugini has said all that needs to be said. I am glad to find that in his last review of the controversy Dr. M. R. James makes no mention of the wrapper evidence.

'WHEN SHALL THESE THREE MEET AGAIN?'

It appears that certain readers have taken the heading of chapter xiv., 'When shall these three meet again?' as an argument for the theory that Drood reappears. If the use of the quotation has any special interest a very good interpretation has been supplied by Mr. Edwin Charles. Mr. Charles points out that the words are used in *Macbeth* before the three witches meet again to plant in Macbeth's mind the tragical lust of ambition. He slays Duncan, who is at once his guest, his kinsman, and his king. And Duncan's sons, also guests of Macbeth, fly respectively to England and Ireland, and Macbeth uses the flight to spread suspicion against them. 'We hear our bloody cousins are bestow'd in England and in Ireland: not confessing their cruel parricide.' Jasper is Edwin Drood's kinsman and guardian and host.

Jasper slays his nephew, and contrives that the suspicion of his murder shall fall on his other guest, Neville Landless, who has to leave Cloisterham. Is this a chance parallel? Does the use of the words in the heading of the chapter prove that Dickens had the tragedy of *Macbeth* in his mind? Mr. Charles not only thinks so, but he holds that the quotation positively destroys any shadow of doubt as to what was intended to be the fate of Edwin. Mr. Charles also notes that Dickens makes another reference to Macbeth in the story when he records the dinner which Grewgious gave to Edwin and Bazzard at Staple Inn. Speaking of the leg of the flying waiter Dickens says that 'it always preceded him and the tray by some seconds, and always lingered after he disappeared,' adding, 'like Macbeth's leg when accompanying him off the stage with reluctance to the assassination of Duncan.'

There is not much to reply to in the argument, but the reply is, to say the least, sufficient.

'EDWIN DROOD IN HIDING'

Another argument has been drawn from the tentative titles written by Dickens here first printed in full. Two of them are 'The Flight of Edwin Drood,' and 'Edwin Drood in Hiding.' On this Mr. Lang writes in the *Morning Post* [130] that, though the titles do not go with the idea that Edwin was to be slain early, Dickens may have intended the titles to mislead his readers, and may have rejected them because he felt them to be too misleading. This I believe to be the exact truth. Dickens was willing to have as much mystery as possible, but he soon perceived that it would not suit his purpose to raise the question whether Edwin was dead or alive.

THE MANNER OF THE MURDER

In Dr. Jackson's book on the subject there is a very able discussion on the manner in which the murder was accomplished. Dr. Jackson inquires: (1) Where and how did Jasper murder Drood, or attempt to murder him? (2) Where and how did Jasper dispose of Drood's body, or attempt to dispose of it? For myself, I believe that the manner of the murder is part of the mystery to be solved as the book proceeds. In this I am in general agreement with Proctor. It would be vain to guess what happened on that stormy night. To give the details definitely would have been to give them prematurely, for much of the interest of the novel is to depend on their unfolding. But certain suggestions may be offered. Dr. Jackson holds that significance is to be attached to Jasper's babblings in the presence of the opium woman. He tells her that he has in his mind the tower of the cathedral, a perilous journey over abysses with an indispensable fellow-traveller. Also that when the journey was really made there was 'no struggle, no consciousness of peril, no entreaty,' but that 'a poor, mean, miserable thing,' which was nevertheless real, lay 'down below at the bottom.' Dr. Jackson thinks that we have here Jasper's confession of the place and the manner of the crime. 'He had ascended the tower with Edwin, and he had seen Edwin's body lying down below, presumably at the foot of the staircase by which they had ascended.'

Mr. Walters thinks that Drood was to be encountered near the cathedral, drugged and then strangled with the black silk scarf that Jasper wore round his own neck. Mr. Proctor and Mr. Lang suppose that Jasper partially strangled Drood near the cathedral, and then deposited his body in the Sapsea monument. They do not explain 'the perilous journey over abysses.' The babblings of the opium den become intelligible if Jasper flung or pushed Drood down the staircase of the tower. But if Drood was attacked outside the cathedral on level ground they are 'unjustifiable mystifications.'

Dr. Jackson further argues that in chapter xii., 'A Night with Durdles,' is a rehearsal of the coming tragedy. He thinks that when Durdles sleeps Jasper makes a wax impression of a key with which Durdles had opened the outside door of the crypt and the door between the crypt and the cathedral. He finds quicklime in the crypt. Then he flings or pushes Drood, who is drugged, down the staircase, and deposits his body in the quicklime in the crypt. Else why did Jasper make a careful study of the tower with Durdles?

My friend and colleague, Miss Jane T. Stoddart, kindly sends me the following:

> Some critics have failed to realise the extreme importance of the Sapsea monument in connection with the murder. It has been suggested by Professor Jackson that Jasper buried the body in a heap of lime in the crypt of the cathedral. But crypts are semi-public places, and if heaps of lime were about workmen would be coming and going. In no case could a corpse lie unnoticed on the open floor of a crypt for more than a few hours. All the evidence points rather to the Sapsea monument in the graveyard as the murderer's chosen hiding-place. Observe how Dickens distinguishes between tombs and monuments, clearly meaning by the latter those massive vault-like erections of stone which are often seen in old churchyards, and which have the dimensions of small chambers with a corridor. Durdles says in chapter V.: "'Say that hammer of mine's a wall—my work. Two; four; and two is six," measuring on the pavement. "Six foot inside that wall is Mrs. Sapsea."
>
> "'Not really Mrs. Sapsea?" asks Jasper.

"'Say Mrs. Sapsea. Her wall's thicker, but say Mrs. Sapsea. Durdles taps that wall represented by that hammer, and says, after good sounding: "Something betwixt us!" Sure enough, some rubbish has been left in that same six-foot space by Durdles's men!"'

There is therefore a 'six-foot' vacant space at least in the Sapsea monument, left, no doubt, for the reception at some far distant date of the Mayor's body. Within this place Jasper decides to deposit the remains of his victim. I do not agree with the critics who fancy there was a Sapsea vault in the crypt. The monument is in the full light of day, for in chapter xii. the Mayor is walking near the churchyard 'on the look-out for a blushing and retiring stranger.' And in chapter xviii. he calls Datchery's attention to this 'small lion' in the churchyard. Mrs. Sapsea, we are distinctly told, is buried within the monument, not in any subterranean vault in the crypt.

THE 'NIGHT WITH DURDLES'

We come now to the night of the mysterious expedition of Jasper and Durdles, when they climb the Cathedral Tower in the moonlight, and when Durdles lies in a drugged sleep on the floor of the crypt. Jasper has been very active during this interval. How has his time been spent? His first business, after possessing himself of the key of the crypt, must have been to search in the bundle carried by Durdles for the key of the Sapsea monument. We have repeatedly been told of his interest in the bundle, into which (see chapter iv.) he had seen Durdles drop this particular key. The inscription had been placed on the monument, but we are to understand that the key had not yet been returned to the Mayor. Having secured this key, Jasper leaves the building, and by some means which can only be conjectured conveys quicklime to the monument, and places it in readiness in the empty space. He may have gone back to the yard-gate where Durdles had showed him the mound of lime, but this would have been a very risky proceeding, as the 'hole in the city wall' occupied by Durdles was beyond Minor Canon Corner, the Monks' Vineyard, and the Travellers' Twopenny. Even in the dead of night, sharp eyes in the lodging-house (Deputy's, for instance) might have seen a man go by wheeling lime in a barrow or carrying it in a sack. It is far more probable that the lime was found nearer to the cathedral.

It has been suggested, further, that Jasper, while away from Durdles, took a wax model of the key of the crypt, which also opens the door at the top of the steps leading from the crypt to the cathedral. The Dean (it is presumed by Professor Jackson) has already entrusted him with another key, that of the iron gate which gives access to the Tower. We are told that Durdles 'bears the close scrutiny of his companion in an insensible way, although it is prolonged while the latter fumbles among his pockets for a key confided to him that will open an iron gate, so to enable him to pass to the staircase of the great Tower.'

Visitors to cathedrals to-day usually find that the key of the tower staircase is in charge of the chief verger, and Jasper would have no difficulty in obtaining a loan of it from this functionary for one night, though hardly for a longer period, as visitors would be coming and going.

Dr. Jackson supposes that the Dean lent his key to the choirmaster, and assumes that, before the expedition with Durdles, Jasper has already taken a wax model of it. If he did so, it must have been in the interval between locking-up time, when we find him (see chapter xii.) conversing with the Dean and the verger, and the time of his changing his coat to go out on the expedition. But Dickens tells us that Mr. Jasper withdrew to his piano, and sat chanting choir music in a low and beautiful voice for two or three hours; 'in short, until it has been for some time dark, and the moon is about to rise.' I take it, then (1) that the iron key was lent to Jasper by the verger for use in this nocturnal expedition; (2) that no wax model of it has been made up to the time of starting; (3) that the verger will look for the return of the key next day.

It seems to me most unlikely that Jasper took a wax model of the crypt key or the key to the iron gate, either on the night of his wandering with Durdles, or at any other time. If he took any wax model, it was that of the key to the Sapsea monument. He used the crypt key merely to let himself out of the building and in again. May not the simplest explanation be that he unlocked the door of the monument, leaving it merely closed, so that a turn of the iron handle would admit him on the night of the murder? According to the picture at the foot of the cover the door seems to have a handle.

I find it difficult to believe that Jasper would order duplicates of two large and unusual-looking keys to be made from wax models by a locksmith in Cloisterham. Such an order would have excited curiosity and perhaps unfavourable surmises in a town where Jasper was so well known. I should expect a curious stare if I carried wax models of church keys even to a locksmith in a London suburb; and Jasper had no time during the week before Christmas to make a journey to London. He was not himself a worker in iron like Roland Graeme in *The Abbot*, who at the cost of much time and labour forged a bunch of keys almost exactly resembling those carried by the lady of Lochleven.

On the night of the murder—that wild and stormy Christmas Eve—Jasper brought Edwin into the churchyard on some pretext, after partially stupefying him with the 'good stuff' which affects the brain so speedily. He may have persuaded him to drink to the dawn of Christmas, as Faust proposed to quaff the cup of poison to the rising Easter dawn:

> Der letzte Trunk sei nun, mit ganzer Seele,
> Als festlich hoher Gruss, dem Morgen zugebracht.

It is after midnight when the murderer and his victim are abroad together. At that hour the 'streets are empty,' and only the storm goes thundering along them. The precincts 'are unusually dark to-night.' No need, then, for Jasper to fear detection as he slips the great silk scarf over Edwin's head and pulls it tightly round his throat. 'No struggle, no consciousness of peril, no entreaty—and yet I never saw that before.'

The maundering talk of Jasper in the opium woman's den need not be taken literally. The difficult and dangerous journey 'over abysses where a slip would be destruction' may have no reference to the actual tower, but to the perils of the scheme and the risk of detection. Among other modes of killing, however, the idea of flinging Edwin from the tower may have occurred to Jasper, and been abandoned. Hence his outcry, 'Look down! look down! You see what lies at the bottom there!'

Dr. Jackson thinks Jasper departed so far from his original plan that he chose the crypt instead of the Sapsea monument as a hiding-place. I think it far more likely that, if ever he intended to hurl Edwin from the tower, he set aside this plan when he found that it meant the making of two duplicate keys. Suppose that in the days following the crime, when the names of Edwin Drood and Jasper were in every mouth in Cloisterham, a small tradesman in some obscure lane were to ask his neighbours why the choirmaster needed these two large keys. The conjecture might be sufficient to destroy him.

I venture to think that Miss Stoddart is right in assigning the place of the body to the Sapsea monument, but I incline to agree with Dr. Jackson that, in order to do justice to the 'Night with Durdles,' and the confessions to the opium woman, we must give some place to the tower as connected with the murder. But I do not understand how Jasper should have seen Drood lying beneath him dead if he had merely pushed him down the tower stairs. Would it not have been more likely that Jasper should have pushed Drood from the galleries, and seen him fall into the space beneath? We cannot lay great stress on the topography of Cloisterham. The Sapsea monument is a pure invention, having no counterpart in Rochester, and Dickens manifestly used the utmost freedom in dealing with his materials. Mr. Lang, by the way, makes a strange mistake in saying, 'As he walks with Durdles that worthy explains (in reply to a question by Jasper) that, by tapping a wall, even if over six feet thick, with his hammer, he can detect the nature of the contents of the vault.' [139] The wall is not six feet thick. The words are: 'six foot inside that wall is Mrs. Sapsea.'

It was for Dickens to explain in the remaining part of the novel how the murder was achieved, and no one has a right to say that he would have failed in doing so. His object is to leave upon us the impression of a murder which was in a singular degree premeditated, ferocious, and complete. If Dr. Jackson is right in supposing that Drood was thrown from the tower, in addition to his being drugged, strangled, and laid in quicklime, Dickens gives us a fresh thrill of horror.

CHAPTER VI—WHO WAS DATCHERY?

In discussing this problem we have no aid from external evidence. It seems that the question was not raised by the critics of the time. We are thrown upon internal evidence, and not only the internal evidence of the book, but the evidence given by a study of Dickens's methods. We have also, as I hope to show, some help given indirectly from Dickens's own biography, and in particular from a book by Wilkie Collins.

It will be convenient at this stage that we should discuss the exact position of affairs after Edwin vanished from the scene.

To us who read the book, Jasper's guilt is so plain and his character so atrocious that we wonder why those who knew him did not at once suspect his guilt. To us Jasper is a self-confessed criminal with his doom already written, but to his neighbours at Cloisterham he presented himself in a wholly different aspect. The Dean himself is not more obviously a pattern of virtuous living. Jasper occupies a conspicuous set of rooms. His fire burns, his red light glimmers, his curtains are drawn, in sight of all the town. He is young, good-looking, socially attractive, and occupied in an almost sacred profession. His duties as choirmaster raise him far above the position of a provincial teacher of music. On Sundays and weekdays the people hear his voice in Psalms and Canticles and Anthems. Edwin expresses the truth about his uncle's standing when he says: 'I should have put in the foreground your being so much respected as Lay Precentor, or Lay Clerk, or whatever you call it, of this Cathedral; your enjoying the reputation of having done such wonders with the choir; your choosing your society, and holding such an independent position in this queer old place.' Mrs. Crisparkle remarks on his 'well-bred consideration,' and his pallor as of 'gentlemanly ashes.' When the story opens there is not a soul in Cloisterham who breathes a word of scandal against him, and his real nature is suspected by only two living persons known to us. One is Rosa Bud, whom he has terrified by his secret love-making; the other the opium woman in London, who has heard strange mutterings in his drugged sleep which to her were not wholly 'unintelligible.' The Dean's fear is that 'Mr. Jasper's heart may be too much set on his nephew.' Nocturnal ramblings with the disreputable Durdles suggest nothing more surprising to the Dean than that Jasper means to write a book about the place. His visits to London are so carefully timed that he is rarely absent from the daily services. He is a favourite with his landlady, Mrs. Tope, and to mothers with marriageable daughters he must appear a very eligible young bachelor.

Who could dream that a man of twenty-six, refined, highly educated, and agreeable, should seek his private recreation in an opium den?

Eight or nine months pass away, and at the point where the story closes Jasper is to all appearance still safe and prosperous. But already the avengers are upon his track, and we shall find it possible from the indications given in the book to show that there were at least six persons designed to have a share in the final capture.

The first mind in which suspicion lodges is clearly that of Mr. Grewgious, and he has taken his impressions of Jasper from Rosa and from Helena Landless. From his interview with Rosa in chapter ix. he learned that the young bride-elect wished to have nothing to do with Jasper. 'I don't like Mr. Jasper to come between us,' she said, 'in any way.' After the murder, when Grewgious comes to Jasper's rooms he has already seen Rosa and Helena Landless, and the latter must have told him of the persecution to which Rosa has been subjected. When Jasper utters a terrible shriek and falls to the ground in a swoon, his companion stands by the fire, warming his hands, and looking curiously at the prostrate figure. He refuses to eat with Jasper, and treats him from that time onwards as 'a brigand and wild beast in combination.' He keeps a personal watch on his movements in Staple Inn, and it is doubtless with his connivance and support that Datchery goes to Cloisterham. Are not these significant words of Grewgious in chapter xxi. to Rosa and Crisparkle: 'When one is in a difficulty, or at a loss, one never knows in what direction a way out may chance to open. It is a business principle of mine, in such a case, not to close up any direction, but to keep an eye on every direction that may present itself. I could relate an anecdote in point, but that it would be premature.' In that last sentence may not Grewgious refer to the plan for sending Datchery to Cloisterham?

When the novel breaks off, Grewgious is working against Jasper, but only on strong suspicion. If Rosa had reported to him Jasper's exact words in her final interview with him, that suspicion may have been heightened to certainty. The part allotted to him in the ultimate crisis is that of identifying the remains of Edwin, now hardly distinguishable otherwise, owing to the action of quicklime in the Sapsea tomb, by means of the ring which was on the young man's person at the time of his murder, and which possessed invincible powers to hold and drag. After giving the ring to Edwin Mr. Grewgious had said 'Her ring. Will it come back to me? My mind hangs about her ring very uneasily to-night. But this is explainable. I have had it so long, and I have prized it so much. I wonder—'

The ring will come back to him from the dust of death.

THE PRINCIPLES OF DISGUISE

It is universally admitted that Datchery was disguised.

Before seeking to identify him with a character already known to us I shall give a short note on the principles and limitations of disguise. Suppose one wishes to disguise himself, how far is it possible for him to succeed? What are the limits within which success is possible?

The question was very carefully discussed in the *Berliner Tageblatt* for 15th May 1912, under the title 'On the Psychology of Dissimulation.' The author, Dr. Hugo Eick, uses the word *Verstellung* entirely in the sense of mental disguise or purposeful deception. In the closing paragraph he limits the possibilities. His remarks on this question are not without value for the students of certain literary problems.

According to Dr. Eick, the really fundamental things which can never be imitated are all manifestations of positive life. For example, we cannot simulate courage, enthusiasm, humility. It is true that we can reproduce certain distinctive marks of courage and enthusiasm which may deceive the inexperienced; but the essence of these qualities can be expressed only by a person who has experienced them, and who possesses them. A brave man may simulate timidity and cowardice, the man who is capable of enthusiasm may wear the mask of apathetic indolence; all depressive and negative conditions may be imitated. But fulness of life and the sap which quickens it cannot be replaced by any dissimulation. The stupid person may persuade another stupid person to believe in his cleverness. But it is impossible to counterfeit cleverness before a clever person unless we possess a minimum of cleverness, because a certain amount of cleverness is needed for the deception itself. The real tone of truth's voice can no more be copied than the fiery gleam of enthusiasm. At this point all the arts of deception fail; the voice contradicts the words. The man who possesses something of these qualities of soul can indeed simulate higher degrees of the same qualities, and can exploit them in unlimited measure. But the elemental things of life are inimitable, and lie beyond the reach of falsehood. He who imitates an elemental thing is immediately discovered—supposing, of course, that the discoverer has himself some share in the element.

THE NECESSARY QUALIFICATIONS

The idea that Datchery is a new character may safely be dismissed. It is in one of the characters already on the stage that we must find Datchery. I might proceed by taking the characters one by one, and by a process of exhaustion arrive at Datchery. But a simpler way may be to enumerate the qualifications required in Datchery, and to show that one character of the story possesses them all. The claims of the other characters may be then discussed.

Datchery is assigned the task of collecting and co-ordinating all the evidence of diverting suspicion from the innocent Neville Landless, and fixing it on the true criminal. In order to do this satisfactorily he required a combination of qualities.

1. We need mental alertness and ability. Stupidity would be fatal.

2. We need high courage and firm resolution.

3. We need an individual who is at once fearless and skilful, one who knows the art of disguise, one who can assume a new character and carry through the assumption to a triumphant end.

4. We need supremely a character whose whole heart goes with the effort at detection. There must be behind all his actions a passionate, personal, intimate concern. These requirements, I believe, are satisfied in Helena Landless, and in Helena Landless alone. The identification is naturally received at first with a certain measure of incredulity and surprise, but a careful and patient study of the story will confirm it.

The theory was put forth by Mr. Cuming Walters in 1905 in his book *Clues to Dickens's 'Mystery of Edwin Drood.'* It is one of the most brilliant conjectures or identifications in literary history. In arguing for its truth I must follow largely on the lines of Mr. Cuming Walters, but I hope to supply some fresh and fortifying considerations.

HELENA LANDLESS

No one will ever understand this problem unless he studies the method of Dickens as explained by Dickens himself in his letter to Wilkie Collins (page 92), and in his reply to the *Edinburgh*, (page 105). Dickens is supremely an artist, and he tries to insert nothing without a purpose. Sometimes his hints are intended to help at the time, sometimes to mislead temporarily. Sometimes they are intended to be plain when the end is reached, and the reader peruses the story in the light of the conclusion.

1. Helena has the mental alertness and ability which qualified her for the task. It is interesting to see from the original manuscript and the proofs how Dickens kept raising and lowering the lights which fell upon the Landlesses. We have seen from the original manuscript in chapter vi. how Dickens heightened his description of the pair. He changed 'A handsome young fellow, and a handsome girl; both dark and rich in colour,' into 'An unusually handsome, lithe young fellow, and an unusually handsome, lithe girl; much alike; both very dark, and very rich in colour.' He emphasises Helena's personal characteristics: 'Slender, supple, quick of eye and limb; half shy, half defiant; fierce of look; an indefinable kind of pause coming and going on their whole expression, both of face and form, which might

be equally likened to the pause before a crouch or a bound.' She fought her way through her tragical childhood, was beaten by a cruel stepfather, and would have allowed him to 'tear her to pieces before she would have let him believe that he could make her shed a tear.' 'She had a masterful look.' Rosa said to her: 'You seem to have resolution and power enough to crush me. I shrink into nothing by the side of your presence.' But it is soon manifest that Helena has a tender heart. She and her brother came to the Crisparkles 'to quarrel with you, and affront you, and break away again.' But they are touched by Mr. Crisparkle's kindness, and Helena is more than touched. Neville tells Crisparkle that in describing his own imperfections he is not describing his sister's. 'She has come out of the disadvantages of our miserable life, as much better than I am as that cathedral tower is higher than these chimneys.' Describing the misery of their childhood to Crisparkle, Neville says: 'You ought to know, to her honour, that nothing in our misery ever subdued her, though it often cowed me. When we ran away from it (we ran away four times in six years, to be soon brought back and cruelly punished), the flight was always of her planning and leading. Each time she dressed as a boy, and showed the daring of a man. I take it we were seven years old when we first decamped.' He says again to Crisparkle: 'You don't know, sir, what a complete understanding can exist between my sister and me, though no spoken word—perhaps hardly as much as a look—may have passed between us.'

2. She has been from the beginning a born planner and leader. She has shown the daring of a man. When her brother lost the pocket-knife with which she was to have cut her hair short, she tried desperately to tear it out or to bite it off. Yet this strong and fiercely passionate girl had herself under the strictest control.

She had no fear of Jasper. Rosa, Helena, Neville, Jasper, and Edwin meet in Crisparkle's drawing-room. Rosa is singing under the control of Jasper. She bursts into tears and shrieks out: 'I can't bear this! I am frightened! Take me away!' Helena immediately comes to the rescue, and with one swift turn of her lithe figure lays the little beauty on a sofa. Edwin says to Jasper:

> 'You are such a conscientious master, and require so much, that I believe you make her afraid of you. No wonder.'

> 'No wonder,' repeated Helena.

> 'There, Jack, you hear! You would be afraid of him, under similar circumstances, wouldn't you, Miss Landless?'

'Not under any circumstances,' returned Helena.

This to my mind is the first unmistakable suggestion of what was to be developed. Here we have Jasper and Helena falling into enmity almost at the first moment of their meeting, challenging one another to battle. Helena accepts the challenge. Not under any circumstances would she be afraid of Jasper. She lives to redeem that word.

3. Dickens expressly tells us that Helena from her childhood was accustomed to disguise herself as a boy. 'When we ran away from it (we ran away four times in six years, to be soon brought back and cruelly punished), the flight was always of her planning and leading. Each time she dressed as a boy, and showed the daring of a man.' This is the strongest reason for the identification of Helena with Datchery. I find it difficult to suppose that any careful student of Dickens will believe that these facts about Helena's disguise were put in without intent. It was one of those facts which Dickens intended his readers to interpret by the backward look. Those who were amazed when Datchery appeared as Helena would be referred back to the significant words which they had missed.

Helena protects her unhappy brother in London, and plans against his enemies. She surmises that 'Neville's movements are watched, and that the purpose of his foes is to isolate him from all friends and acquaintances, and wear out his daily life grain by grain.' She secures the help of Mr. Tartar.

In her conference with Grewgious, Helena plans for checkmating Jasper, and inquires whether 'it would be best to wait until any more maligning and pursuing of Neville on the part of this wretch shall disclose itself, or to try to anticipate it.'

4. Helena's whole heart went with the effort at detection. We have seen her hatred of Jasper. In the conversation between Helena and Rosa about Drood and Jasper, Rosa betrays her horror of Jasper and his mesmeric power over her, which makes her ashamed and passionately hurt. They resume on the same strain.

> Says Rosa:
>
> 'But you said to-night that you would not be afraid of him, under any circumstances, and that gives me—who am so much afraid of him—courage to tell only you. Hold me! Stay with me! I am too frightened to be left by myself.'
>
> The lustrous gipsy-face drooped over the clinging arms and bosom, and the wild black hair fell down protectingly over the childish form. There was a slumbering gleam of fire in the intense dark eyes, though they were then

softened with compassion and admiration. Let whomsoever it most concerned look well to it!

This last sentence is another of the unmistakably prophetic sentences in Dickens. Helena was the sworn champion thenceforth of Rosa against Jasper. Helena submits herself to the fairy bride and learns from her what she knows. When Jasper is mentioned and Rosa says, 'I could not hold any terms with him, could I?' Helena answers with indignation, 'You know how I love you, darling. But I would sooner see you dead at his wicked feet.'

As to the close and tender affection between Helena and Neville, and her vehement sympathy with his trial, there is no question. I quote one passage because it seems to me a most striking fact that in the proofs of Dickens the whole of it is struck out:

> 'I don't think so,' said the Minor Canon. 'There is duty to be done here; and there are womanly feeling, sense, and courage wanted here.'
>
> 'I meant,' explained Neville, 'that the surroundings are so dull and unwomanly, and that Helena can have no suitable friend or society here.'
>
> 'You have only to remember,' said Mr. Crisparkle, 'that you are here yourself, and that she has to draw you into the sunlight.'
>
> They were silent for a little while, and then Mr. Crisparkle began anew.
>
> 'When we first spoke together, Neville, you told me that your sister had risen out of the disadvantages of your past lives as superior to you as the tower of Cloisterham Cathedral is higher than the chimneys of Minor Canon Corner. Do you remember that?'
>
> 'Right well!'
>
> 'I was inclined to think it at the time an enthusiastic flight. No matter what I think it now. What I would emphasise is, that under the head of Pride your sister is a great and opportune example to you.'
>
> 'Under *all* heads that are included in the composition of a fine character, she is.'
>
> 'Say so; but take this one. . . . She can dominate it even when it is wounded through her sympathy with you. . . . Every day and hour of her life since Edwin Drood's

disappearance she has faced malignity and folly for you as only a brave nature well directed can. So it will be with her to the end . . . [pride] which knows no shrinking, and can get no mastery over her.'

Immediately after, Neville says: 'I will do all I can to imitate her.'

'Do so, and be a truly brave man, as she is a truly brave woman,' answered Mr. Crisparkle stoutly. In his proof Dickens struck out the words, 'as she is a truly brave woman.'

It is impossible, I think, to read this and not to see that Dickens is afraid that we may too soon suspect Helena Landless of being Datchery.

Neville's sufferings under the suspicion are unmistakable and cruel. When Crisparkle saw him he wished that his eyes were not quite so large and quite so bright. 'I want more sun to shine upon you.' Neville tells him that he feels marked and tainted even when he goes out at night, and he never goes out in the day. He says, though Dickens did not mean us to read the sentence: 'It seems a little hard to be so tied to a stake, and innocent; but I don't complain.'

Such are the main reasons that induce me to believe that Helena is Datchery. It is admitted on all hands that she was meant to play an important part in the story. What part does she play if she is not Datchery?

DATCHERY'S WISTFUL GAZE

But the proof that impresses me as much as any other is to be found in the passage: 'John Jasper's lamp is kindled and his lighthouse is shining when Mr. Datchery returns alone towards it. As mariners on a dangerous voyage, approaching an iron-bound coast, may look along the beams of the warning light to the haven lying beyond it that may never be reached, so Mr. Datchery's wistful gaze is directed to this beacon and beyond.' The detective of whom this is written cannot possibly be a mere detective. His heart is engaged in the search. This fits Helena, and Helena only, of all the characters that have been brought forward. A professional detective paid by Grewgious could never have behaved in that way. Helena's whole heart was in the business. She had to relieve her fondly-loved brother from a cruel weight of anxiety and suspicion. She had to bring a villain whose baseness she thoroughly knew to justice. She had to liberate the girl friend she loved from persecution, and she looked to a beyond, to the haven—the haven of Crisparkle's love.

DATCHERY'S WIG

Datchery wears a wig, and it is unusually large, as though a woman's hair were concealed under it. As Mr. Cuming Walters also points out, Helena undoubtedly had a strong motive for not sacrificing her hair to the disguise, for she was unmistakably in love with Crisparkle.

DATCHERY'S HANDS

There is no doubt that if Datchery was Helena, one of her chief difficulties must have been with her hands.

Miss Stirling Graeme, the author of *Mystifications*, had a marvellous power of disguising herself. 'There was nothing extraordinary about her,' says Dr. John Brown, 'but let her put on the old lady; it was as if a warlock spell had passed over her; not merely her look, but her nature was changed: her spirit had passed into the character she represented; and jest, quick retort, whimsical fancy, the wildest nonsense flowed from her lips, with a freedom and truth to nature which appeared to be impossible in her own personality.'

Sir Walter Scott in his *Journal* for 7th March 1828 tells us that when she returned to her party in the character of an old Scottish lady she deceived every one. 'The prosing account she gave of her son, the antiquary, who found an auld wig in a slate quarry, was extremely ludicrous, and she puzzled the Professor of Agriculture with a merciless account of the succession of crops in the parks around her old mansion-house. No person to whom the secret was not entrusted had the least guess of an impostor, *except one shrewd young lady present, who observed the hand narrowly, and saw it was plumper than the age of the lady seemed to warrant.*'

In the *Daily Mail* of 4th April 1912 there is an account of two girls who lived together, passing as husband and wife. The man with whom they lodged said: 'The husband's hands were so small and soft that both my wife and myself were suspicious.'

I ask the attention of readers to the manner in which Dickens refers to Datchery's hands. I do not lay too much stress on these indications, but they deserve consideration.

1. We read in chapter xviii. about Datchery in the coffee-room of the Crozier, 'as he stood with his back to the empty fireplace waiting for his fried sole, veal cutlet, and pint of sherry.' ('Empty' was an afterthought on Dickens's part.) Here we have Datchery keeping his hands out of view.

2. A little after, Datchery asks the waiter to take his hat down for a moment from the peg. If he had stretched out his own hand it might have been noticed.

3. Later in the same chapter, when Datchery meets Jasper and the Mayor, he does not shake hands with them. '"I beg pardon," said Mr. Datchery, making a leg with his hat under his arm.' Originally this was written 'hat in

hand.' If he carried his hat under his arm, one hand would be buried in the hat.

4. Afterwards we read of Datchery following Jasper and the Mayor, 'with his hat under his arm, and his shock of white hair streaming in the evening breeze.'

5. When Datchery is talking to the opium woman, 'he lounges along, like the chartered bore of the city, with his uncovered grey hair blowing about, and his purposeless hands rattling the loose money in the pockets of his trousers.' His hands are thus out of sight. Immediately after we find him 'still rattling his loose money,' and again, 'still rattling.'

6. At last he begins to count out the sum demanded of him by the opium woman. 'Greedily watching his hands, she continues to hold forth on the great example set him.' Of course, she may merely be watching for the money in his hands, but there may be something more in it than this. Let it be noted that Dickens originally wrote, 'Greedily watching him,' and inserted 'his hands' later.

7. Immediately after 'Mr. Datchery drops some money, stoops to pick it up.' In all the scene with the opium woman he keeps his hands out of sight as much as possible, and when he does show them they strike the old woman.

I may add, though much has been said about the possibility of detecting by means of the voice, this does not appear by any means to be impossible, or even very difficult. Only one meeting between Jasper and Helena is recorded. Her voice is described as low and rich. Even if he had talked with Datchery, it is more than doubtful whether he would have known the voice again, music-master though he was. Datchery, if our supposition is right, was an expert in disguise, and could have carried it off. I find in the pleasant *Recollections and Impressions* of Mrs. Sellar that she had no difficulty in deceiving her nearest friends. She tells us how one day, when Sir David and Lady Brewster were dining with the Sellars at St. Andrews, after dinner Lady Brewster begged her to dress up and take in Sir David:

"'But what will account for my absence?'"

"'Oh, you have been obliged to go to bed with one of your headaches; and I'll introduce the stranger.'"

'So I went upstairs, put on a false front, and was announced as Miss Craig. On the gentlemen coming in I was specially introduced to Sir David, but not being at all attractive-looking, he soon left me for younger and fairer friends! Determined he should take some notice of me, I said I would not play the piano unless Sir David asked me; and on this being told him he

muttered: "God bless the woman! what does she mean! I don't know her."'
[163]

Mr. Lang says: 'A young lady of my acquaintance successfully passed herself off on her betrothed as her own cousin—also a young lady—and Dickens had not to imagine anything so unlikely as that.'

To this I may add that Scott tells a story of Garrick and his wife. Mrs. Garrick was an accomplished actress, but once she witnessed an entertainment in which was introduced a farmer giving his neighbours an account of the wonders seen on a visit to London. The character was received with such peals of applause that Mrs. Garrick began to think it rivalled those which had been so lately lavished on Richard the Third. At last she observed her little spaniel dog was making efforts to get towards the balcony which separated him from the facetious farmer. Then she became aware of the truth. 'How strange,' she said, 'that a dog should know his master, and a woman, in the same circumstances, should not recognise her husband!' [164a]

THE ORIGIN OF DICKENS'S IDEA

So strong is the evidence for Helena Landless being Datchery that even the chief advocates of the Proctor theory have fully admitted its force. Dr. M. R. James says: 'I will go as far as this: if Edwin is dead, then Datchery is Helena.' [164b] Mr. Andrew Lang over and over again admitted that Datchery might be Helena. But he contended that, if so, the idea of Dickens is improbable with the worst sort of improbability, is terribly far-fetched, and fails to interest. 'It is the idea of a bad sixpenny novel. We are asked to credit Dickens with the highest scientific skill, and this egregious invention is the result of his science. The idea would have been rejected by Mr. Guy Boothby. But it does not follow that Mr. Walters has not hit on Dickens's idea. If he has, *Edwin Drood* is far below *Count Robert of Paris* in its first uncorrected state, as the public will never know it.'

There is something in this argument, and it has never yet been fairly met, but I believe that I can show that the idea was probably suggested to Dickens by one figure in real life, and another figure in fiction. So far as I am aware these suggestions are made for the first time.

In the *Bancroft Recollections*, Lady Bancroft writes on page 31:

> My first part at the Strand Theatre was Pippo, in his burlesque *The Maid and the Magpie*, which proved an immense success, and I established myself as a leading favourite. It was not until the *Life of Charles Dickens* was published that I knew his opinion of this performance.

Dickens had written years before, in a letter to John Forster, these words:

'I went to the Strand Theatre, having taken a stall beforehand, for it is always crammed. I really wish you would go to see *The Maid and the Magpie* burlesque there. There is the strangest thing in it that ever I have seen on the stage—the boy Pippo, by Miss Wilton. While it is astonishingly impudent (must be, or it couldn't be done at all), it is so stupendously like a boy, and unlike a woman, that it is perfectly free from offence. I never have seen such a thing. She does an imitation of the dancing of the Christy Minstrels—wonderfully clever—which, in the audacity of its thorough-going, is surprising. A thing that you *cannot* imagine a woman's doing at all; and yet the manner, the appearance, the levity, impulse, and spirits of it are so exactly like a boy, that you cannot think of anything like her sex in association with it. I never have seen such a curious thing, and the girl's talent is unchallengeable. I call her the cleverest girl I have ever seen on the stage in my time, and the most singularly original.'

Lady Bancroft adds: 'Charles Dickens's being impressed with my likeness to a boy reminds me that on the first night I acted in *The Middy Ashore*, one of the staff came up to me at the wings and said: "Beg pardon, young sir, you must go back to your seat; no strangers are allowed behind the scenes."' From this it must be inferred that Dickens had there that evening a new idea as to the possibilities of disguise. Dickens's letter was written in 1859.

I believe that Dickens in this Datchery assumption was mainly influenced by Wilkie Collins. Most writers on Dickens have observed his admiration for Collins, the way in which he co-operated with him, and the high value he placed on his work. *The Moonstone* has been referred to in this connection, but I venture to think that the novel which led Dickens to his idea was *No Name*. I have already printed (page 91) Dickens's wildly enthusiastic testimony to its merits. He placed it far above *The Woman in White*, and far above *The Moonstone*. In particular, he admired the character of Magdalen Vanstone.

In *No Name* we are introduced to a charming family—husband, wife, and two daughters—the Vanstones. Then it turns out that the parents are unmarried. The husband made a great mistake in marrying a bad woman in his early youth, and is nearly ruined in consequence. He induces a good woman to live with him as his wife, and he has a fortune of £80,000. By a singular mischance both he and the mother die suddenly about the same time. Vanstone had made a will leaving his property to the daughters, but just before the death of his wife he discovers that his real wife is dead, and so they go out and get married. The law is that marriage abolishes all past wills. The consequence is that the will is not effective, and the two daughters are left without a penny, and without a name. What are the girls to do? The younger, Magdalen, has great force of character, and shows a talent for the stage. She resolves to revenge herself on her father's brother who has taken all the money. Instead of going to work as an ordinary actress, she gives performances of her own. She is very clever at acting different parts. She disguises herself as an old woman, and in all sorts of disguises. She is nineteen, almost the age of Helena Landless. Here is a description of the way in which she disguises herself:

> I found all the dresses in the box complete—with one remarkable exception. That exception was the dress of the old north-country lady; the character which I have already mentioned as the best of all my pupil's disguises, and as modelled in voice and manner on her old governess, Miss Garth. The wig; the eyebrows; the bonnet and veil; the cloak, padded inside to disfigure her back and shoulders; the paints and cosmetics used to age her face and alter her complexion—were all gone. Nothing but the gown remained; a gaudily flowered silk, useful enough for dramatic purposes, but too extravagant in colour and pattern to bear inspection by daylight. The other parts of the dress are sufficiently quiet to pass muster; the bonnet and veil are only old-fashioned, and the cloak is of a sober grey colour. But one plain inference can be drawn from such a discovery as this. As certainly as I sit here, she is going to open the campaign against Noel Vanstone and Mrs. Lecount, in a character which neither of those two persons can have any possible reason for suspecting at the outset—the character of Miss Garth.
>
> What course am I to take under these circumstances? Having got her secret, what am I to do with it? These are awkward considerations; I am rather puzzled how to deal with them.
>
> It is something more than the mere fact of her choosing to disguise herself to forward her own private ends that causes my present perplexity. Hundreds of girls take fancies for disguising themselves; and hundreds of

instances of it are related year after year, in the public journals. But my ex-pupil is not to be confounded, for one moment, with the average adventuress of the newspapers. She is capable of going a long way beyond the limit of *dressing herself like a man, and imitating a man's voice and manner*. She has a natural gift for assuming characters, which I have never seen equalled by a woman; and she has performed in public until she has felt her own power, and trained her talent for disguising herself to the highest pitch. A girl who takes the sharpest people unawares by using such a capacity as this to help her own objects in private life; and who sharpens that capacity by a determination to fight her way to her own purpose which has beaten down everything before it, up to this time—is a girl who tries an experiment in deception, new enough and dangerous enough to lead one way or the other, to very serious results. This is my conviction founded on a large experience in the art of imposing on my fellow-creatures.

I say of my fair relative's enterprise what I never said or thought of it till I introduced myself to the inside of her box. The chances for and against her winning the fight for her lost fortune are now so evenly balanced that I cannot for the life of me see on which side the scale inclines. All I can discern is, that it will, to a dead certainty, turn one way or the other on the day when she passes Noel Vanstone's doors in disguise.

I am not prepared to criticise Dickens's plot as Mr. Lang has done. If Wilkie Collins made an admirable heroine of Magdalen Vanstone disguising herself variously, why should not Dickens succeed in making a character as wonderful and more attractive of Helena Landless? There is nothing to be condemned in the idea itself. It has been used by masters, and used successfully. There would have been nothing to condemn, I believe, in Dickens's way of working it out if he had lived to complete his book. The comparison with Guy Boothby is singularly inept.

OBJECTIONS

The objections that have been made to the Datchery-Helena theory turn mainly on the supposed disgracefulness of Dickens deceiving his readers as he did, and working out a melodramatic idea. These objections might have been, and, I believe, would have been, scattered to the winds by the complete story.

The most serious objection to the identification of Datchery as Helena is the confusion in the chronology. This is admirably stated by Dr. Jackson, who examines in a masterly way the arrangement of the chapters. He comes to the conclusion that chapter xviii. has been introduced prematurely. It ought to have followed chapter xxii. If Dickens had lived to issue the fifth and sixth monthly instalments, he would have placed our chapter xviii. without the alteration of a single word after chapter xxii., next before chapter xxiii. We know that Dickens told his sister-in-law that he was afraid the Datchery assumption in the fifth number was premature. Dr. Jackson gives us a full and valuable examination of the manuscript so far as its arrangement is concerned. I have tested his statements in every point, and can only confirm them. To Dr. Jackson's chapter ix., 'The Manuscript,' I refer the reader.

There are other objections. In particular, some are troubled by Datchery's masculine ways. They ask how Helena, fresh from Ceylon, should have known the old tavern way of keeping scores. There is not much in this. In fact, these scores, which could have served no purpose, seem to me the natural expression of a buoyant girl rejoicing in her achievements. A cool-headed, middle-aged detective would never have expressed himself in such a way. Why should not Helena have known about tavern scoring? She was accustomed to walk with her brother Neville, and in the course of their walks they may very likely have visited a tavern now and then. We read of Neville finding his way to a tavern when he walked away that dark night. In *Phineas Finn*, at the end of chapter lxxi., Trollope, reporting the conversation of two high-born ladies, Lady Laura Kennedy and Miss Violet Effingham, has this:

> 'Was I not to forgive him—I who had turned myself away from him with a fixed purpose the moment that I found that he had made a mark upon my heart? I could not wipe off that mark, and yet I married. Was he not to try to wipe off his mark?'

> 'It seems that he wiped it off very quickly; and since that he has wiped off another mark. One doesn't know how many marks he has wiped off. They are like the innkeeper's score which he makes in chalk. A damp cloth brings them all away, and leaves nothing behind.'

This shows, at least, that chalk-marking is not a matter of esoteric knowledge in England, but is known to high and low. I may note that Dickens inserted the adjective 'uncouth'—'a few uncouth, chalked strokes'—over his original manuscript, to make it clear no doubt that the scorer was an amateur at the business.

Then there are objections to Datchery's masculine fare—fried sole, veal cutlet, and pint of sherry; bread and cheese, and salad and ale. It must be remembered that Helena was in disguise. This was not a mere disguise of dress, but it was a disguise of everything. She was assuming a character and carrying it out. She had all the ability and all the will for accomplishing this. In doing masculine things she was simply carrying out her disguise. A woman passing for a man must do what a man would do or she will fail, and be found out.

It has been suggested that if Datchery is Helena, and therefore knows the Gatehouse, why does she give it 'a second look of some interest'? Dr. Jackson replies very well that the house for her has now a new importance, and is the object upon which her thoughts are to be concentrated for weeks, and perhaps for months. But Dickens did not mean this passage to be printed, for good reasons of his own.

WHAT DICKENS DID NOT MEAN US TO READ

This leads us to note that certain passages which have been much discussed were not meant for publication by Dickens. That is, he struck them out in proof. Dr. Jackson points out that in chapter xviii., when Datchery consults the waiter at the Crozier about 'a fair lodging for a single buffer,' he is obviously asking to be recommended to Tope's. The waiter is puzzled at first. When Mr. Datchery asks for 'something venerable, architectural, and inconvenient,' the waiter shakes his head. 'Anything cathedraly, now?' Mr. Datchery suggested. Then comes the mention of Tope. Datchery boggles about the cathedral tower seeking for lodgings, but Dickens did not mean us to read the words: 'With a general impression on his mind that Mrs. Tope's was somewhere very near it, and that, like the children in the game of hot boiled beans and very good butter, he was warm in his search when he saw the tower, and cold when he didn't see it.'

When the Deputy pointed out Jasper's, first Dickens wrote '"Indeed?" said Mr. Datchery, with an appearance of interest.' Then he wrote: '"Indeed?" said Mr. Datchery, with a second look of some interest.' Then he struck out the sentence entirely.

Dickens also struck out the sentence which describes Datchery after the Deputy left him: 'Mr. Datchery, taking off his hat to give that shock of white hair of his another shake, seemed quite resigned, and betook himself whither he had been directed.' He also struck out the passage in which Mrs. Tope and Datchery talk of what occurred last winter:

> Perhaps Mr. Datchery had heard something of what had occurred there last winter?

Mr. Datchery had as confused a knowledge of the event in question, on trying to recall it, as he well could have. He begged Mrs. Tope's pardon when she found it incumbent on her to correct him in every detail of his summary of the facts, but pleaded that he was merely a single buffer getting through life upon his means as idly as he could, and that so many people were so constantly making away with so many other people as to render it difficult for a buffer of an easy temper to preserve the circumstances of the several cases unmixed in his mind.

Nearly all the conversation between the Mayor and Datchery is deleted. See page 9.

Also Dickens erases the little talk between the Deputy and Datchery beginning: 'Master Deputy, what do you owe me?' See page 11.

It may not be possible to deduce any assured inference from these omissions, but they are worth pondering, and may be referred to again.

CHAPTER VII—OTHER THEORIES

THE DROOD-DATCHERY THEORY

One opposing theory is that Datchery was Drood. With all respect for the scholars who have propounded it, this appears to me a purely comic notion. It is the most fantastical of all fancies as to who was Datchery. As Dr. Blake Odgers points out, every one at Cloisterham knew the murdered man: a mere white wig would be no disguise at all. I may add that if Jasper had discovered him he would almost be justified in finishing the murder this time. For what would be Drood's object? The theory is that, in spite of his being drugged, throttled, perhaps thrown from a tower, at all events buried in quicklime, and in all probability locked up in the tomb, Drood got away when his uncle was triumphantly flinging his watch and scarf-pin into the river. Supposing it were so, what was Drood doing while he watched his uncle? Is it said that he was so bemused by the opium that he did not know who had handled him in such a murderous fashion? This is very hard to believe. Mr. Andrew Lang himself says: 'Fancy can suggest no reason why Edwin Drood, if he escaped from his wicked uncle, should go spying about instead of coming openly forward.' Mr. Archer says the flaw is that the theory provides no motive whatever for Drood's disguising himself as Datchery. Why should Drood devote himself to an elaborate scheme of revenge upon his near kinsman and friend? He would want to hush the matter up, and save Jasper from himself. Why did Drood let Neville lie under the suspicion of murder, and why was not Rosa let into the secret? It is hardly worth while to point out that there is nothing in Drood's character as given us which could have enabled him to show the ability, the composure, and the self-control of Datchery. Who could have supplied him with money to live idly at Cloisterham? His money was all locked up till he came of age, and Jasper was his guardian and trustee. If Grewgious supplied the money, why did not Grewgious make an end of Neville's misery?

THE BAZZARD-DATCHERY THEORY

A far more plausible theory is that Datchery was Bazzard. Dickens almost invites readers to connect Bazzard with Datchery when he makes Grewgious say to Rosa when she came up to London that Bazzard 'was off duty here altogether just at present, and a firm downstairs with whom I have business relations lend me a substitute.' (The words 'here altogether' were added by Dickens.)

I have no doubt that Dickens in some way meant to explain Bazzard's business. But that Bazzard should have been Datchery will appear a sheer impossibility to careful students of Dickens. Proctor, whose side remarks are often excellent, puts the point briefly as follows: 'No one at all familiar with Dickens's method would for a moment imagine that Datchery is Bazzard, Mr. Grewgious's clerk. Bazzard was as certainly intended to come to grief, and be exposed in the sequel as was Silas Wegg in *Our Mutual Friend*.'

Mr. Cuming Walters says: 'Literary art rebels against the idea. Bazzard was one of Dickens's favourite low comedy characters.'

Dr. James dismisses the Bazzard theory 'because Buzzard in his first and principal appearance has too much both of the fool and of the knave about him to develop into the Datchery whom we are intended to admire.'

Dr. Jackson says: 'Capacity can ape incapacity, but incapacity cannot ape capacity. This being so, I am sure that Bazzard, who is not only "particularly angular, but also somnolent, dull, incompetent, egotistical, is wholly incapable of playing the part of the supple, quick-witted, resolute, dignified Datchery."' In these judgments I agree. Bazzard has no ethical quality. He has not the smallest personal interest in the discovery. How could it be said of Bazzard that his 'wistful gaze is directed to this beacon, and beyond?'

As the theory is obvious and popular, it may be worth while to say something more, and Dr. Hugo Eick's words, as previously quoted, may help us. Helena Landless had the elemental qualities needed for the Datchery role. Note that among Shakespeare's heroines who masquerade as men, Rosalind, in *As you Like It*, and Julia, in *Two Gentlemen of Verona*, have not these elemental qualities and are suspected. Portia has them, and even her own husband does not know her in her doctor's robes. She is recognised by all as a young doctor, but not one person in court thinks 'There is a woman!' Bazzard might have imitated depressive and negative conditions, but he could not have imitated the qualities of positive life. 'Fulness of life and the sap which quickens it cannot be replaced by any dissimulation.'

It should also be noted that if Bazzard was Datchery, he had no occasion to disguise himself in a huge white wig, for he was not known in Cloisterham.

THE GREWGIOUS-DATCHERY THEORY

The theory that Datchery was Grewgious may be dismissed in a sentence. Grewgious with his 'awkward and hesitating manner,' his 'shambling walk,' his 'scanty flat crop of hair,' his 'smooth head,' his 'short sight,' his general angularity fits in no way the watchful, courtly, adroit, fluent, and versatile Datchery.

THE DATCHERY-NEVILLE THEORY

Mr. Lang has a wild conjecture somewhere that Neville was Datchery, and that Helena was disguised as Neville. It is difficult to treat this seriously. Neville would inevitably have been found out. His cause was undertaken by his friends, and his business was to study and wait. Why on earth should Helena disguise herself as Neville?

THE TARTAR-DATCHERY THEORY

There is something more attractive about this theory, and it has been very well argued by Mr. G. F. Gadd in the *Dickensian*, vol. ii. p. 13. Mr. Gadd uses the argument 'with a second look of some interest,' as showing Datchery's ignorance of Cloisterham. He quotes Tartar's phrase 'being an idle man,' as corresponding with the 'idle buffer living on his means.' He suggests that Dickens at this point of his story avails himself of the licence not unfrequent in fiction of temporarily abandoning the strictly chronological order. He suggests that Tartar as a seafaring man might know something of opium smoking, and compares the wistful gaze directed to this beacon and beyond, to what is said about Tartar as he and Rosa entered his chambers at Staple Inn. 'Rosa thought . . . that his far-seeing eyes looked as if they had been used to watch danger afar off, and to watch it without flinching, drawing nearer and nearer.'

But, as Dr. Jackson points out, Tartar has his duties assigned to him. He has to watch over Neville and see him almost daily. Again, Tartar does not know about Cloisterham and the Drood mystery what Datchery knows and needs to know. 'Thirdly, I doubt whether the cheery, straightforward, simple-minded Tartar is capable of Datchery's versatility, subtlety, and address.' To this I add that Tartar's heart is not engaged in the business as Helena's is. Also what need is there for his disguise? He has never been in Cloisterham, and nobody there knows him.

For these reasons we conclude that Helena and no other is Datchery. I have taken no account of the theory that Datchery is an unknown person. An unknown person could not possess the necessary qualities of heart.

CHAPTER VIII—HOW WAS 'EDWIN DROOD' TO END?

How *Edwin Drood* was to end is a problem which can only be solved to a certain extent. We find we are left in the middle, and as much mystery remains as fully justifies the title. We do not know the precise manner in which the murder was accomplished. In particular, we are left ignorant as to the way in which the crime is to be brought home to the victim. We cannot define the relations of the opium woman to Drood and Jasper and the Landlesses. We do not know the history of Jasper's early years. We can do no more than speculate, and the speculations must be confined within strict limits. The first question is, whether Dickens himself knew how he was going to extricate and complete his narrative.

Scott has left us the astonishing statement [184] that 'I have generally written to the middle of one of these novels without having the least idea how it was to end.' Mr. Skene, a true friend of Sir Walter Scott, tells us [185] that when Scott described to him the scheme which he had formed for *Anne of Geierstein*, he suggested to him that he might with advantage connect the history of René, king of Provence, in which subject Skene had special means of helping him. Scott accepted the suggestion, 'and the whole *dénouement* of the story of *Anne of Geierstein* was changed, and the Provence part woven into it, in the form in which it ultimately came forth.'

Was Dickens in the same case when death interrupted him in his work?

Was this an 'apoplectic' novel?

Scott speaks frankly of *Count Robert of Paris* and *Castle Dangerous* being his 'apoplectic books.' Does *Edwin Drood* bear the same relation to the body of Dickens's work as *Count Robert of Paris* and *Castle Dangerous* bear to the Waverley Novels? Mr. Lang, whose views on this subject varied much, in one of his later writings takes the view that Dickens was deeply embarrassed. He says: 'It is melancholy to think of this great and terribly overtasked genius tormented by fears that were only too real.' He finds the story wandering on, living from hand to mouth, full of absurdities. He thinks that Dickens was very capable of changing his original purpose, and saving the life of Edwin.

There is no doubt that Dickens was puzzled about the order of his chapters. Forster tells us that Dickens 'became a little nervous about the course of the tale from a fear that he might have plunged too soon into the incidents leading on to the catastrophe such as the Datchery assumption (a misgiving he had certainly expressed to his sister-in-law).' I have already expressed agreement with Dr. Jackson in his plan for renumbering the chapters. Unless this plan is adopted there is chronological confusion. Also there is no doubt that Dickens had been working under terrific strain. But the testimony of those who knew him best is that his faculties were never brighter and stronger than they were in his last months.

The same impression is left upon me by his unfinished novel. Those who dislike Dickens's later manner may easily find faults. They may say that Honeythunder is grotesque rather than amusing. They may say that Jasper's courtship of Rosa is melodramatic and wolfish. I confess to being perpetually puzzled by the account of Neville's capture on the morning after the murder. Why was he pursued in that manner? All that was known against him was that he had been with Edwin on the previous night. He is only eight miles away from Cloisterham, and stopping at a roadside tavern to refresh. He starts again on his journey, and becomes aware of other pedestrians behind him coming up at a faster pace than his. He stands aside to let them pass, but only four pass. Other four slackened speed, and loitered as if intending to follow him when he should go on. The remainder of the party (half a dozen, perhaps) turn and go back at a great rate. Among those who go back is Mr. Crisparkle. Nobody speaks, but they all look at him. Four walk in advance and four in the rear. Thus he is beset, and stops as a last test, and they all stop. He asks:

> 'Why do you attend upon me in this way? . . . Are you a pack of thieves?'
>
> 'Don't answer him,' said one of the number. . . . 'Better be quiet. . . .'
>
> 'I will not submit to be penned in,' says Neville; 'I mean to pass those four in front.'

They all stand still, and he shoulders his heavy stick and quickens his pace. The largest and strongest man of the number dexterously closes with him and goes down with him, but not before the heavy stick has descended smartly. Naturally Neville is utterly bewildered. Two of them hold his arms and lead him back into a group whose central figures are Jasper and Crisparkle. Why on earth did not Crisparkle speak to him at the beginning, and tell him what had happened? All this is somnambulistic.

There seems to be a slight slip in chapter ii.

Jasper's room at the Gatehouse is described. It has an unfinished picture of a blooming schoolgirl hanging over the chimneypiece. At the upper end of the room Mr. Jasper opens a door and discloses a small inner room pleasantly lighted and prepared for supper.

'Fixed as the look the young fellow meets is, there is yet in it some strange power of suddenly including the sketch over the chimneypiece.' They dine in the inner room. The cloth is drawn, and a dish of walnuts and a decanter of rich coloured sherry are placed upon the table.

'How's she looking, Jack?'

Mr. Jasper's concentrated face again includes the portrait as he returns: 'Very like your sketch indeed.'

'I am a little proud of it,' says the young fellow, glancing up at the sketch with complacency, and then shutting one eye, and taking a corrected prospect of it over a level bridge of nut-crackers in the air.

Dickens seems to have forgotten that the sketch is in the other room.

It seems to me that these are slips, but I do not find any other readers have taken the same view. With these exceptions, the story seems to be one of Dickens's best books. Its grasp of local colour and detail is as strong as ever it was. There is much of his old humour in the Mayor, in Miss Twinkleton's Girls' School, in Billickin, in Durdles and his attendant imp. Also the story is constructed with the greatest care and ingenuity. Any one who carefully goes over the manuscript and the proofs will see that Dickens had a plan in his mind that he half revealed and half concealed, that his phrases and details are chosen with the nicest care, and that he meant to reward those who at the end could take a 'backward look' by the delight they would experience in seeing how everything had been scrupulously planned and artistically conducted to a climax. We cannot do justice to the book in its present state. But Dickens's royal genius was at its full, and would have vindicated itself. He had set himself deliberately to carrying out a plot far more exact than he had ever attempted, and the end was in view from the beginning.

This is not to say that the reason of every incident and every description was disclosed from the first. I have previously discussed Edgar Allan Poe's reading of *Barnaby Rudge*, and shown that his perception, keen as it was, yielded him less than he thought. I have shown how Dickens prepared the plan for *Little Dorrit* from the start of his book. It may be traced now, but without the 'backward glance' it would not have been easy to trace it.

We may also say with some confidence that no new characters of importance would have been introduced to us in the second half. In the chapter 'Half Way with Dickens' I have shown that this is the case with five of his principal books. The conclusion is not stringent, for Dickens was free to change his method. But it may be said to be highly probable; if it is true we are left to conjecture the part that the various characters would have played in the winding up of the tale.

The book was to end with the capture and conviction of Jasper. I have already written of the part played and to be played by Grewgious. Another hunter of Jasper was Durdles. The task assigned to Durdles among the hunters is fairly clear. Sooner or later, by tapping round the Sapsea monument he is to discover the presence of 'a wheen banes,' or at least of some unsuspected 'rubbish.' He had put the inscription on the monument before Christmas, and had no doubt satisfied himself then that all was safe. 'When Durdles puts a touch or a finish upon his work, no matter where, inside or outside, Durdles likes to look at his work all round, and see that his work is a-doing him credit.'

Having made his inspection when the epitaph was put on, Durdles would have no further curiosity about the tomb until, in the following summer, he took Mr. Datchery on a rambling expedition as he had taken Jasper. His peculiar gift, like that of the bloodhound, is to aid in tracking down the quarry.

Deputy has also his part to play. From the first Jasper hates and fears Deputy, and there are signs near the close of *Edwin Drood* that this strange boy, who has some characteristics in common with Dickie Sludge, of *Kenilworth*, is to form a close alliance with Datchery. The ugliest side of Jasper's character displays itself in his treatment of the 'young imp employed by Durdles.' The chanting of the line, 'Widdy Widdy Wake-cock warning,' has for him a note of menace. With the fury of a devil he leaps upon the boy when he emerges from the crypt with Durdles, and hears a sharp whistle rending the silence. 'I will shed the blood of that impish wretch!' he cries; 'I know I shall do it.' Durdles has to appeal to him not to hurt the boy. 'He followed us to-night, when we first came here,' says Jasper. 'He has been prowling near us ever since.'

Deputy denies both accusations. 'I'd only just come out for my 'elth when I see you two a-coming out of the Kinfreederal.'

What has Deputy actually seen? He may have testimony to give of the most vital consequence, but even if he has seen nothing of Jasper's movements while Durdles lies asleep, or of his approach to the Sapsea monument, he will tell Mr. Datchery of that furious onslaught when Jasper clutched his throat and threatened to kill him. He will prove a very useful ally of the hunters.

It seems quite inconceivable that either Durdles or Deputy could have known the whole secret and kept it. Neither of them was capable of keeping a secret long. But they might have suspicions, and they might and would know circumstances which when rightly interpreted led to the inevitable conclusion.

I cannot but think that the chief part in the coming narrative was to be played by the opium woman. The novel from the very first page has a touch of the East. In Wilkie Collins's *The Moonstone* the Indians did their part, and then vanished from the scene. But in *Edwin Drood* we have the Landlesses from Ceylon with a touch of dark blood, or at least of the Eastern spirit. Mr. Lang is in excess of the facts when he calls them Eurasians, and Dickens hesitates in ascribing black blood to them. They are more probably gypsies. We have also the connection of Edwin Drood with the East. There is more than a suggestion of dark blood in John Jasper. Above all, we have the opium woman. What was the connection between John Jasper and the opium woman? What was John Jasper's history before he came to Cloisterham?

We do not know, but conjectures have been hazarded. Mr. Cuming Walters thinks that the opium woman's hatred of Jasper may be due to the fact that Jasper has wronged a child of the woman's. He also conjectures that Jasper may be the son of the opium woman. Dr. Jackson conjectures that Jasper seduces a young girl who had treated the old woman kindly, that he neglected this girl for Rosa, that the girl committed suicide, and that the old woman devoted herself to the pursuit of the betrayer. All this is mere speculation. We have really no means of judging whether the speculation is true or not. It does seem that the woman's peculiar hatred of Jasper must have an origin and a grave cause. Miss Stoddart suggests that the opium woman was not wholly degraded, and that she is horrified by Jasper's continually repeated threatenings while under the influence of opium; that her sympathies have been wakened for that hapless Ned who bears a threatened name, and she resolves to do her best to serve him. With an honest purpose she makes her way before Christmas to Cloisterham. She loses sight of Jasper, but actually meets Edwin Drood. The kind act of that young stranger causes her to unload her conscience, and she bids him be thankful that his name is not Ned. At her second visit in the summer she knows from Jasper's confessions under her own roof that the long premeditated crime has actually taken place, and her object in visiting Cloisterham is to gather evidence that may serve the ends of justice. This sunken creature has a task assigned to her, and she fulfils it.

I am not sure that Dickens means to throw any redeeming light on the character of the opium woman. She has been wronged; she is seeking vengeance, and at last, she finds it. How this comes to pass Dickens meant to tell us, but he meant, no doubt, to surprise us in the telling.

My own belief is that Dickens intended to surprise his readers by telling them of some unsuspected blood relationship between his characters. Surprises of this kind are given in his novels. No reader of *Oliver Twist* could have guessed from the first part Oliver's relationship to Monks and the Maylies. Who would have supposed from the first half of *Nicholas Nickleby* that Smike was the son of Ralph?

> 'That, boy,' repeated Ralph, looking vacantly at him.
>
> 'Whom I saw stretched dead and cold upon his bed, and who is now in his grave—'
>
> 'Who is now in his grave,' echoed Ralph, like one who talks in his sleep.
>
> The man raised his eyes, and clasped his hands solemnly together:
>
> '—Was your only son, so help me God in heaven!'
>
> In the midst of a dead silence Ralph sat down, pressing his two hands upon his temples. He removed them after a minute, and never was there seen, part of a living man undisfigured by any wound, such a ghastly face as he then disclosed.

Again, who would have supposed from the early part of *Great Expectations* that Estella was the daughter of Abel Magwitch? [196]

In *Barnaby Rudge*, Maypole Hugh turns out to be an illegitimate son of Sir John Chester. In *The Old Curiosity Shop*, 'The Stranger' is found to be the brother of the Grandfather. In *Bleak House*, Esther Summerson is revealed as a daughter of Lady Dedlock. In *Our Mutual Friend*, John Rokesmith turns out to be John Harmon.

That the action of opium had a part to play in the revelation can hardly be doubted. The whole book is drenched in opium. In *The Moonstone* the problem is who stole the jewels. It is solved by opium. The jewels are stolen by a man under the influence of opium surreptitiously administered. He is quite unconscious of what he has done, and remains unconscious. Afterwards he is discovered by a fresh administration of opium. When the opium has completely done its work the man repeats his deed, and the experiment is conclusive.

I do not think that any one reading right on would name the perpetrator of the theft, and yet when we take a backward glance we find an account of a dinner-party about the seventieth page which gives the clue. I doubt whether any one on first reading it would see in it anything that mattered, and yet it contains everything that matters. The height of art in work like this is to conceal art. You may be able at an early stage to introduce facts which contain the ultimate solution of your problem, and yet appear important enough to be stated for their own sake. The solution of the problem, or rather the materials of the solution, should be given, and yet the reader should be unable to detect the full significance of the preliminary statement till the complete clearing arrives. At the same time the book will not be satisfactory if details are superfluous, if they do nothing to carry one on to the dissipation of the mystery.

It is not to be denied that this fitting of everything into its place is at times a little wearisome. 'The construction is most minute and most wonderful,' wrote Anthony Trollope of Wilkie Collins. 'I can never lose the taste of the construction. The author seems always warning me to remember that something happened at exactly half-past two on Tuesday morning, or that a woman disappeared from the road just fifteen yards beyond the fourth milestone.' There is truth in this, but if Anthony Trollope had written a novel of mystery, which perhaps he could never have done, he would have had to take the same path.

Another doctor in *The Moonstone* tells us that the ignorant distrust of opium in England spreads through all classes, so much so, that every doctor in large practice finds himself every now and then obliged to deceive his patients by giving them opium under a disguise. He himself claims that opium saved his life. He suffered from an incurable internal complaint, but he was determined to live in order to provide for a person very dear to him. 'To that all-potent and all-merciful drug I am indebted for a respite of many years from my sentence of death.'

Like Collins, Dickens was keenly interested in the possibilities of opium. Collins himself was a lavish consumer of the drug, but I do not think it has been suggested that Dickens himself ever touched it. Nor is it likely, for Dickens with all his tenseness of nerve was an eminently self-controlled and temperate man. But in *Edwin Drood* he has inserted a sentence in praise of opium. The opium woman says to Datchery: 'It's opium, deary. Neither more nor less. And it's like a human creetur so far, that you always hear what can be said against it, but seldom what can be said in its praise.' The last sentence was an afterthought on the part of Dickens. It has been written in.

As to whether Jasper was made ultimately to repeat his crime in any fashion under the influence of opium, it is impossible to say. He was unquestionably more or less under the influence of the drug when he committed it.

The literary men of Dickens's period were much interested in the action of drugs, in mesmerism, and the like. Elliotson, to whom *Pendennis* is dedicated, was on intimate terms with Dickens. Dickens plainly implies that Crisparkle went to the weir because Jasper willed him to do so. Collins and Dickens were both addicted to calling witnesses to their accuracy. At the close of *Armadale*, Collins says: 'Wherever the story touches on questions connected with law, medicine, or chemistry, it has been submitted before publication to the experience of professional men. The kindness of a friend supplied me with a plan of the doctor's apparatus—I saw the chemical ingredients at work before I ventured on describing the action of them in the closing scenes of this book.' Every one remembers the 'spontaneous combustion' preface to Bleak House. I do not know whether any medical man can be found to confirm the science of *Armadale*, or of *Bleak House*, or of *The Moonstone*. But that is not the question before us. We have only to do with what the novelist himself believed to be a scientific possibility. In *Kenilworth* [200] Wayland compounds 'the true Orvietan, that noble medicine which is so seldom found genuine and effective within these realms of Europe.' Scott adds a note: 'Orvietan, or Venice treacle, as it is sometimes called, was understood to be a sovereign remedy against poison; and the reader must be contented, for the time he peruses these pages, to hold the same opinion, which was once universally received by the learned as well as the vulgar.' Dickens's science must be received in the same manner.

Mr. Crisparkle has one piece of evidence in his memory. 'Long afterwards he had cause to remember' how, when he entered Jasper's rooms and found him asleep by the fire, the choirmaster 'sprang from the couch in a delirious state between sleeping and waking, and crying out, "What is the matter? Who did it?"'

As we have already seen, the gathering of the threads is in the strong hands of Datchery.

As we know, Forster adds that Neville Landless was to have perished in assisting Tartar finally to unmask and seize the murderer. It will be seen that this part of his testimony is more doubtful than the rest, and cannot, therefore, be so implicitly accepted, but it may well be true. Melancholy seems to mark Neville Landless for its own, and his passion for Rosa is hopeless. If he dies, it is a heavy blow for his devoted sister, who finds her triumph marred by the death of her brother. Singularly enough, some writers who have hesitated to accept Forster's more expressed testimony make much of the death of Neville Landless and its circumstances. It need only be pointed out that all this is pure conjecture, however ingenious it may be.

I find no difficulty in believing that Dickens carried out his plan of making Jasper give in prison a review of his own career. This has been called a poor and conventional idea, but as worked out by Dickens it would neither have been poor nor conventional. What remains to be told is, I repeat, largely the story of John Jasper's earlier life.

Milton Keynes UK
Ingram Content Group UK Ltd.
UKHW030625061024
449204UK00004B/295